VICTORIAN TECHNOLOGY AND ITS PRESERVATION IN MODERN BRITAIN

NORMAN A. F. SMITH

A Report
submitted to the Leverhulme Trust

LEICESTER UNIVERSITY PRESS
1970

VICTORIAN TECHNOLOGY
AND ITS PRESERVATION IN
MODERN BRITAIN

Two week loan
Benthyciad pythefnos

Please return on or before the due date to avoid overdue charges
A wnewch chi ddychwelyd ar neu cyn y dyddiad a nodir ar eich llyfr os
gwelwch yn dda, er mwyn osgoi taliadau

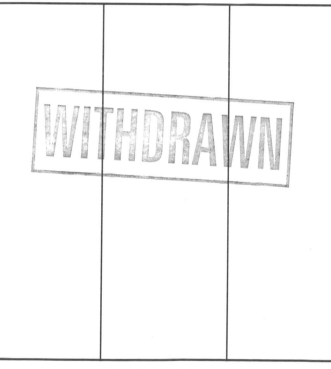

CONTENTS

SUMMARY   vii

PREFATORY NOTE   viii

INTRODUCTORY STATEMENT: Industrial Conservation
  by Professor Jack Simmons   ix

THE VICTORIAN TECHNOLOGY SURVEY   1

Origins   3

Form and aims of the Victorian Technology Survey   4

Procedure   6

History of technological preservation   7

What has already been conserved   11
    Railway locomotives   12
    Road vehicles   13
    Aviation   13
    Stationary prime movers   14
    Machine tools   14
    Models   15
    Craft industries   15
    Textile technology   17
    Mining   18
    Metals   18

What should be conserved   20
    Shipbuilding and ships   20
    Agricultural technology   21
    Electronics   21
    Civil engineering   22
    Chemical technology   23
    Heavy engineering   24
    Plans, documents and drawings   24
    Pottery and glass making   26
    Leather trades   27
    Printing and paper making   27

Agencies and procedures   28

Current projects 33
   Birmingham 33
   Bristol 34
   Leicester 34
   Manchester 35
   Coventry 35
   Bradford 36
   Dudley 36
   North-east England 36
   Lea Valley 37
   Ironbridge 37

Conclusions and recommendations 38
   1. *Organization* 38
   2. *Regionalism* 41
   3. *Publicity* 41
   4. *Finance* 42
   5. *Temporary storage* 44

What needs to be done 44

Priorities 46

APPENDICES
  I Technological Preservation in the Bath–Bristol Region *by Dr R. A. Buchanan* 49

  II Technological collections in Great Britain 59

  III Two examples of preservation by means of Private Trusts 70

  IV The major Technological Museums under development 73

The cover design by James Dexter shows an impression of one of the set of beam engines at the Abbey Pumping Station, Leicester, site of the projected Museum of Technology for the East Midlands.

SUMMARY

This Report embodies the findings of the Victorian Technology Survey which was carried out by the Department of Science and Technology at Imperial College, London. The Survey was designed to investigate the problems of preserving the technology of Victorian Britain. The first part of the Report comprises an explanation of the Survey's origins followed by an outline of the history of technological preservation and some details of other surveys carried out by the Confederation of British Industry and the Industrial Monuments Survey.

Three of the Victorian Technology Survey's basic aims were to discover what specimens of Victorian technology have already been preserved and how well, what else should be preserved, and what agencies and procedures exist to promote preservation. These three questions are answered in the relevant sections of the Report.

At the present time there are numerous plans for more preservation in new museums and these projects are reviewed in the section entitled "Current Projects".

There follow the conclusions reached by the Survey. This section is subdivided under the headings Organization, Regionalism, Publicity, Finance and Temporary Storage.

At the end of the Report are four Appendices containing lists and details of existing and proposed museums plus some information on particular preservation issues.

PREFATORY NOTE

The materials on which this Report is based have been compiled by Norman A. F. Smith, who also wrote the first draft. This draft was then revised by A. Rupert Hall and submitted to the Steering Committee for comment and criticism. The Report was then further modified in the light of the Steering Committee's knowledge and opinions.

We are most grateful to Professor Jack Simmons for his splendid statement of the necessity for technological conservation which we have printed as an Introduction to this Report; and also to Dr R. A. Buchanan for his detailed survey of the problem in the region of Bristol and Bath, which we print as Appendix I. Similar surveys could be, and in part have been, prepared for the whole country. Dr Buchanan's survey shows clearly the urgency of protecting immovable "industrial monuments".

Further, we are most grateful to all the members of the Steering Committee for their advice, learning and criticism; their names appear at the end of the Report as testimony to the fact that they have approved its content.

A. RUPERT HALL
Professor of the History of Science and Technology
Imperial College, London

NORMAN A. F. SMITH
Principal Investigator
Department of the History of Science and Technology
Imperial College, London

INTRODUCTORY STATEMENT

Industrial Conservation

by

Professor Jack Simmons

The systematic recording and preservation of our industrial heritage is interesting for its own sake, but it has a wider and deeper importance too. It would generally be agreed that this country has made at least three outstanding contributions to the thought and life of the world as a whole. The first has been through her literature—through Shakespeare and the Authorized Version of the Bible, for instance, through Byron and Scott and Dickens. The second is in the form of political thinking and the institutions resulting from it—the writings of Locke and John Stuart Mill, parliamentary government. The third is in commerce and technology.

It was in the mid-eighteenth century that Britain began to make her outstanding contribution to the industrial development of Europe and the world. In the 1760s and 1770s French visitors to this country came to appreciate the superiority of some branches of Britain's industrial techniques and production, and to urge the importance of this lesson upon their government. It heeded their advice to some extent and encouraged William Wilkinson to establish ironworks near Nantes and coke-smelting plant at Le Creusot; whence, in 1789, he went on to develop coke-smelting in Prussia. In the closing years of the *ancien régime* in France, English textile machinery was being imported on a large scale—larger, indeed, than the French government knew, for much of it was smuggled. For the first time, in these years, the name of an English manufacturer became widely known throughout the western world. The name was Josiah Wedgwood's; this earthenware made its way all over Europe, from Sweden and Russia to Italy and Spain, into the East and the West Indies and into North America.

The French Revolution, and the long wars in which Britain was engaged with France, halted this process; but they also opened up new avenues for British trade, into South America and the Eastern

Mediterranean. When peace came in 1815 British industrial production, stimulated by the demands of the war, was poised to capture the markets of the world; and for the next sixty years Britain enjoyed an unquestionable supremacy in manufacturing industry and in the technology needed for its development. It is, approximately, in these two generations that she made her greatest gift to the material civilization of the world.

But if that gift is to be appreciated rightly, it must be seen in the context of what preceded it and what followed. Its roots lie in the eighteenth century—in some matters they reach back further still; and the achievement did not come to an end at one point, in the 1870s or at any other time. Britain's railway service was still an example to the rest of the world, in speed and in its consideration for all classes of the people, in 1890; at the turn of the century she wrought a revolution in shipping through the development of the marine turbine; in the hands of Courtauld's Britain leapt forward in the production of artificial silk in 1900–1914.

The British people themselves have been somewhat blind to their own achievement. Their interest was fixed at the outset entirely on the task itself, and on the commercial activity it ministered to and engendered; then they were inclined to take it for granted, with a good deal of dangerous complacency. It is only now, when most elements of the old supremacy have disappeared, that they are beginning to appreciate the magnitude of the achievement of their forebears, and to wish to observe and understand it for its own sake. It is no accident that "industrial archaeology", though not in fact a wholly new study, has come to win recognition during the past fifteen years, when we are starting to see the nineteenth century in a clearer light and more complete perspective.

But recognition has come at the eleventh hour—in some cases at its fifty-ninth minute, or after twelve o'clock has struck. For the visible evidence of this great achievement of the past has been in the course of very rapid destruction, and that continues all around us today. This is not due solely to the obsolescence of the older machinery, equipment, and buildings, though that is an important part of the process. It has to be remembered that Britain is still paying the price of her early arrival at industrial maturity, standing at a disadvantage in comparison with many of her competitors, who have been able to launch themselves with superior equipment. At least equally important, in this process of destruction, have been the swift changes of ownership and control that have overtaken every branch of industry in the course of the last thirty years and are still continuing vigorously. They often involve the closure of well-equipped works in the interest of a concentration of activities in one very large centre, and the destruction of records to an extent that will never be able to be measured. If we do not take action quickly, many most important examples of machinery and equipment will have gone, with the irreplaceable records that can alone explain them in economic, and so in true historical, terms.

This is in no sense a plea for preservation for its own sake. It is a plea for a highly selective and intelligently planned scheme of preservation, designed to keep only those things that are really important, in one of three ways. They may be originators. They may be essential links in the chain of evolution. Or they may be important as examples, not of what was novel but of what was the norm, the thing in ordinary, everyday use; this last category is often the hardest to illustrate.

For the great bulk of the interesting objects, which have to be destroyed, we must rely on the industrial archaeologists to record them as meticulously as possible, principally through the medium of the Industrial Monuments Survey.

As far as preservation is concerned, what is needed is surely a tripartite enterprise: a planned schedule of preservation, industry by industry; careful protection, in properly constituted record offices, for all the many related documents; adequate provision for housing all that is to be preserved, both in London and in the provinces. If this is not achieved, we shall fail signally in what is a clear and prime duty to succeeding generations. We shall also be false to our forebears, whose energy, skill and courage gave Britain the eminent place she has occupied in the world.

THE
VICTORIAN TECHNOLOGY
SURVEY

ORIGINS

There is at the present time a growing interest in and concern over Great Britain's industrial and technological history and the problem of ensuring that proper attention is given to conserving something of this past for the benefit and interest of posterity. Early in 1968 the discussions of a number of parties interested in this matter were given particular cogency by the concurrence of two impending events—the then projected closing of St Pancras Station, and that of the British Railways Transport Museum at Clapham. If a new Museum of Victorian Technology were to be founded in London— as some proposed—then it seemed that the former building might provide a suitable home for it and the latter a number of important exhibits.

However, it was not then clear either that (a) the foundation of a new museum in London would be the best possible step to take; or (b) St Pancras Station would necessarily be its optimal site. Finally, detailed questions of what would be involved in founding such a new museum were not examined, nor was information available about the number, type or importance of Victorian technical relics that might be displayed in a new museum. All concerned felt that further knowledge of (a) what ought to be conserved, and (b) what conservation activities were already in being, would be useful.

Since then, the picture has altered to the extent that St Pancras Station is no longer available, British Railways having announced its indefinite use as a railway station. Hence the questions "Would it be proper to found a new museum of Victorian technological history?" and "Should a museum, if it were founded, be in central London?" need no longer be confused by discussions of the future use of a particular structure or site.

In March 1968, one of those principally concerned in these discussions, Lord Murray of Newhaven, asked the Department of the History of Science and Technology at Imperial College, London, to undertake a pilot survey of activities directed towards the conservation of surviving remains of Victorian technology in modern Britain, and of the magnitude of the problem of further conservation. The required funds were most generously provided by the Leverhulme Trust Fund and the Victorian Technology Survey began on 1 August 1968.

FORM AND AIMS OF THE
VICTORIAN TECHNOLOGY SURVEY

The Survey was carried out under the direction of Professor A. Rupert Hall, Head of the Department of History of Science and Technology at Imperial College, and the principal investigator was Dr Norman A. F. Smith. The Survey's work was guided by a Steering Committee comprising the following ten people:

Dr R. A. Buchanan (Bath University of Technology)
Sir Arthur Elton, Bt (Chairman of the Council of the Centre for the Study of Industrial Archaeology at Bath University)
Mrs Jane Fawcett (Victorian Society)
Sir David Follett (Science Museum)
Professor A. Rupert Hall (Imperial College)
Dr M. B. Hall (Imperial College)
Mr J. Pope-Hennessy, C.B.E. (Victoria and Albert Museum)
Professor Jack Simmons (University of Leicester)
Dr Norman A. F. Smith (Imperial College)
Mr Rex Wailes (Industrial Monuments Survey)

The Steering Committee met on 5 August 1968 to discuss the form and aims of the Survey. It was agreed that the term "Victorian" should be interpreted broadly, covering the period from 1815 to 1914 at the very least, with no restrictions on earlier and later years when relevant to a proper assessment of the problem. Of all historical fields technology is characterized by continuous and steady development, so much so that classification into discrete periods is not only difficult but even misleading because it obscures the origins of ideas and overlooks their consequences. The decision to treat the term "Victorian" flexibly has proved to be the right one.

The Victorian Technology Survey has been directed towards three main objectives:

1. Finding out what particular examples of Victorian technology have been conserved and how well.
2. Finding out what else should be conserved, especially in those branches of technology where little or no attention has been given to conservation so far.
3. Examining the agencies and procedures which exist to find, restore and preserve significant relics.

It was also agreed by the Steering Committee that there were certain things which the Survey was *not* required to do:

1. To locate suitable specimens. In the time and with the resources available this would have been impossible. As will be emphasized later, the business of finding relics is a specialized operation best left to indviduals and groups each concerned with small areas.

2. To take up particular causes. At any moment numerous important and well-known monuments of technological history are in danger, e.g. at present the Iron Bridge at Coalbrooke-dale, Shropshire. The preservation of each of these individual relics is a deserving cause, but the Survey could not become involved in the particular details of one or all of them without impairing its overall view of the problem.

3. To involve itself in any preservation schemes as such. Having no money or authority, the Survey was not in a position to undertake any preservation itself or to become involved in any precise schemes for museums or the like.

There are two distinct preservation problems, relating to things which are immovable and those which are movable. This division is the first and obvious one when one begins to classify types of technical relics.

(1) *Immovable*. This category includes such items as bridges, dams, canal works, industrial buildings, furnaces, shipyards, mines and quarries, some types of steam engine, water-mills and wind-mills.

Many of these are not strictly speaking incapable of being moved. In principle windmills, industrial buildings, bridges and dams could be re-established at another place with the expenditure of a huge amount of time, effort and money. Occasionally this may be desirable, and it has sometimes been done. But generally the term immovable is sensibly true and it must also be recognized that by moving some objects all their historical significance is lost. There would not be much value in preserving an old tide mill, for instance, at an inland site.

(2) *Movable*. This category comprises two distinct parts:

(a) Hardware such as machinery, tools, equipment, engines etc. Many such items are small and their removal to a museum is the only way of ensuring their survival. The same is true for larger items, such as heavy machinery, once their working life is over. However, removing large specimens to a museum is neither easy nor cheap and once there, the problems of re-erection are significant; a lot of space is required and very heavy loads must be borne by the museum's floors.

(b) Documentary records such as plans, drawings, surveys, photographs, accounts, letters and so on. These constitute a special but nonetheless important part of the picture. They are of great interest to the economic as well as the technical historian. But they are at the same time very vulnerable because of the ease of their destruction when a business closes down. Moreover, technical libraries become vulnerable once they cease to be relevant to contemporary needs. Documentary records are a vital technical record in many cases because they often disclose information which cannot be determined from physical remains.

PROCEDURE

Initially some time was spent examining the nature of technical preservation through existing literature: publications such as *Industrial Archaeology*; books on industrial archaeology and the history of technology; the *Museums Journal*; *Museums and Galleries of Great Britain and Ireland*; the *Libraries, Museums and Art Galleries Yearbook*; and so on. It was decided to tackle the investigation along five main lines:

1. By seeking the aid of individuals known or suspected to have experience and/or information relevant to the inquiry.
2. By consulting existing bodies such as industrial archaeology societies, railway societies, history societies and the like.
3. Through museums; not only those whose main business is the preservation of technical relics, but also those which have departments of technical history or even isolated specimens.
4. Through universities and colleges whose interests cover industrial archaeology and/or the history of technology, and which may therefore be in a position to aid preservation.
5. Through industry in whose possession must be many specimens suitable for preservation.

These were the ways in which the Victorian Technology Survey attempted to uncover the information it was looking for. The existence of the Survey was given publicity by publishing a short description of its aims in the following places:

Museums Association *Monthly Bulletin*
The Victorian Society *Newsletter*
Technology and Culture
The Newcomen Society *Bulletin*
Industrial Archaeology
The Bulletin of Local History

HISTORY OF TECHNOLOGICAL PRESERVATION

The idea of assembling collections of historic technological equipment is much older than might be imagined. It dates back at least to the beginning of the seventeenth century when Francis Bacon in *The New Atlantis* (published posthumously in 1627) put forward Utopian ideas for a museum of inventions and portraits of inventors. Nothing was done at the time. In 1761 the Society for the Encouragement of Arts, Manufactures and Commerce held an industrial exhibition but this did not become permanent.

In the U.S.A. in 1793 the notion was introduced that all patent applications should be accompanied by models and that these should ultimately form a part of a technical collection of the National Museum. Also in the U.S.A., the Smithsonian Institution in 1881 received a large collection of specimens from the Centennial Exhibition held in Philadelphia in 1876.

In France the Conservatoire des Arts et Métiers, founded in 1794, formed its collections around two nuclei: the collection of machines assembled by Vaucanson and the one-hundred-year-old collection of scientific apparatus put together by the Académie Royale des Sciences.

Owing to the environment engendered by the Industrial Revolution there was in Great Britain at the beginning of the nineteenth century a great lay interest in mechanics. By the mid-nineteenth century the concept was current that a museum should have as its aim the advancement of knowledge, a notion already accepted in France.

In this country a fresh impetus sprang from the Great Exhibition of 1851. The surplus of exhibits left over from the Exhibition was used to establish the South Kensington Museum in 1857 under the patronage of Prince Albert. The aim was to "promote the application of art to industry and to illustrate the progress and development of science". A distinct attitude can be detected in that merely collecting items was not the aim but rather it was held that a collection should have some educational or instructive value.

Under the guidance of Bennett Woodcroft the South Kensington Museum eventually evolved into the Science Museum. Woodcroft, however, not only gathered together items typical of current technical and scientific work. He deliberately looked for historical relics and thanks to his endeavours the Science Museum acquired such things as Watt's beam engine of 1777, the Lap engine of 1788, "Puffing Billy", the "Rocket" and Bell's reaper.

It is worth noting that museum items which are now of historic interest were not necessarily acquired as such. When first exhibited for educational purposes they were "modern" pieces of equipment. On the other hand Woodcroft himself saved a number of machines from the scrap-heap and in this sense shared the problems which face present-day curators trying to create technical collections which illustrate historical developments.

Despite its name the Science Museum is the finest "technical" museum in the world, the Deutsches Museum of 1906 in Munich being its only rival. Interest in technical museums, however, is shared by other countries, notably the U.S.A., France, Sweden, Holland, Austria and Italy.

Prior to the Second World War three other technical museums were opened in Great Britain: the Railway Museum at York which emerged from the centenary celebrations of the Stockton and Darlington Railway in 1925; the Museum of Science and Engineering founded in Newcastle-upon-Tyne in 1934; and the Holman Museum at Camborne especially concerned with Cornish Engines. That interest in technical history is rapidly on the increase is evident from the rate at which museums of technology have sprung up in the period since 1945. A great many are listed in Appendix II; among the more important are the Birmingham Museum of Science and Technology, the Canal Museum at Stoke Bruerne, museums of transport at Swindon, Clapham, Glasgow and Belfast, and the Museum of English Rural Life at Reading. The list of existing museums and of those for which plans have been drawn up is impressive and indicates immediately that a good deal has already been achieved.

An important conservation activity of more recent years has

been the preservation *in situ* of industrial monuments, notably wind- and water-mills. The first windmill to be deliberately preserved in this way, as the result of a public subscription, was that on Wimbledon Common (1868).

The Victorian Technology Survey is not the first attempt at an assessment of the problems pertaining to technical preservation. In June 1959, the Council for British Archaeology (CBA) formed a Steering Committee for Industrial Archaeology. In December of the same year a conference was held by the CBA at which the Ordnance Survey and the Ministry of Public Building and Works were represented. The County of Stafford appointed an Archaeological Officer to organize a pilot-survey of industrial monuments in Staffordshire. The Ministry of Public Building and Works decided to await results of this survey before taking steps to preserve industrial monuments.

The Research Committee on Industrial Monuments, set up in 1959 by the CBA, decided to publish a Handbook of Industrial Archaeology. The aim of the handbook was to get important monuments recognized, listed, documented and, where possible, preserved. The publication never appeared in this form but the material was used in the preparation of Kenneth Hudson's well-known book *Industrial Archaeology*, published in 1963.

In 1962 the CBA persuaded the Treasury to provide funds for an Industrial Monuments Survey (the IMS). In April 1963 the Survey officially began its work under the joint sponsorship of the Ministry of Public Building and Works and the CBA. Mr Rex Wailes was appointed to run the IMS, as a full-time consultant. Mr Wailes' brief was three-fold:

1. To advise on the conduct of a national survey of industrial monuments.
2. To enable an assessment to be made quickly by the Government as to what steps should be taken to record and preserve industrial monuments.
3. To advise the Ministry on urgent cases where immediate action was required.

The official definition of an industrial monument was: "any building or other fixed structure—especially of the period of the Industrial Revolution—which either alone or in association with plant and equipment, illustrates or is significantly connected with the beginnings and evolution of industrial and technological processes, including means of communication".

One consequence of the IMS has been the creation of the National Record of Industrial Monuments (NRIM) which is supervised by Dr R. A. Buchanan at the Centre for the Study of the History of Technology in Bath. Contributors to the Record include various individual researchers, numerous local societies, libraries, museums and other groups. So far the coverage of the NRIM has been uneven geographically, varied in quality and the contributions have ranged from obviously important items to the very trivial. Indeed some well-known and important monuments have not yet appeared in the Record.

It seems that one of the NRIM's initial purposes—the provision of essential data for implementing preservation—has not been fulfilled. This is because there is a time-lag between field recording and the appearance of the information in the NRIM during which time the items may be destroyed; further, if no record of an industrial monument is made then the NRIM can do nothing towards its preservation. On the other hand it does seem that the NRIM will ultimately result in a most comprehensive list eventually of great value as an archive. It has of course no official authority, nor financial resources, to facilitate its interest in conservation.

In May 1966 the Ministry of Public Building and Works announced that the Confederation of British Industry (CBI) was to "help in the task of tracking down and preserving outstanding industrial monuments". The basic idea was that industry itself should play an important rôle in preserving its own heritage. The Ministry of Public Building and Works contemplated the preservation only of outstanding examples, because of the cost and possible hindrance to industrial development which might otherwise result. Two basic problems emerged:

1. Industrialists are often totally unaware of the value and interest of some of their obsolete plant.
2. Industry finds it hard to reconcile the notion of preservation with the need to modernize.

There was also a financial problem because under the conditions of "severe economic restraint" (which still prevail) money was hard enough to find for expansion and modernization, much less preservation.

A small Steering Committee was set up in 1966. The CBI agreed to channel the recommendations of individual industries to the Ministry of Public Building and Works. In fact it proved to be difficult, in some cases very difficult, to rouse enthusiasm. Two industries, the iron and steel and the brewing industries, were especially sympathetic and so were a few others. The CBI Steering Committee reported that at least some progress had been made towards rousing interest and putting aside basic prejudices but nothing more has resulted. However, one of the fruits of this Committee's activity has been the preservation of the flint-grinding mill at Cheddleton in North Staffordshire; see Appendix III (II).

The Victorian Technology Survey differs from the above two enquiries in several respects. The CBI's work was concerned only with the rôle that industry itself could play and was probably handicapped for that reason. Industry is highly suspicious of history. The IMS is concerned with a particular sort of technical relic, that is, industrial monuments and their associated equipment, and is not restricted to any one period. By contrast the Victorian Technology Survey is limited, more or less, to a given period but within that period has endeavoured to deal with the technical spectrum throughout its whole width. An ambitious objective perhaps, but at least the Victorian Technology Survey has been completed and has drawn conclusions.

WHAT HAS ALREADY BEEN CONSERVED

Initially we hoped that it would be possible to analyse existing collections with a view to showing in some detail what sort of technical relics exist and which branches of technology have to date received most attention. In fact a quantitative answer is not possible because the necessary catalogues do not exist. The major technical museums in Great Britain of course possess inventories of their own contents but in the case of the big museums their analysis would be a major operation. Another problem is the existence of technical collections or even single items, frequently very important, in museums which are not well known for technology even though they may be recognized as important in other fields. The difficulties do not end there. There are also private collections, either truly private in the sense of collections in the possession of individuals, or collections held by industry, sometimes large companies but often very small firms. The fact is that it is not even possible to be sure that a complete list of all the existing technical collections has yet been compiled (see Appendix II) and the preparation of a complete national catalogue would be a monumental undertaking, probably impossible. The initial idea that the Victorian Technology Survey should compile such an analysis was therefore quickly abandoned. One influential museum curator reported that the preparation of a catalogue of technical relics of a special type in a local area had proved to be beyond him. That is some measure of the extent of the problem at present. It is to be hoped that ultimately a comprehensive catalogue will be prepared and published but it will not be in the immediate future and the urgent problem of current preservations must proceed without such a list.

By visiting museums, of all types and not just those devoted to technology, by examining the relevant literature and discussing the question with experts, a qualitative picture of those fields which have been particularly well covered can be drawn. The position is set out here under subject headings.

Railway locomotives

It is estimated that close to four hundred railway locomotives are at present in various states of preservation in Great Britain. These comprise mainly "dead" or stationary specimens which are never put in steam and in some cases are beyond the stage where they ever could be. They range from the imposing and beautifully cared for examples in the Science Museum, in the various railway museums and a few other places, to rusting wrecks which were acquired with the best intentions but whose satisfactory maintenance has subsequently proved to be beyond the resources of their entirely genuine but somewhat over-ambitious owners. A proportion of steam locomotives are kept at work on privately owned and operated systems such as the Tal-y-lyn Railway, the Bluebell Line and the recently inaugurated Dart Valley Railway. These locomotives are well cared for and in good condition—the fact that they are used is insurance of this. To what extent is the operation of old steam locomotives an example of technical preservation? It appears often to be a bonus. Enthusiasts, it seems, like to "play trains" and the public are willing to finance their activities and there is nothing wrong with either. The question remains, though, whether the collection of railway locomotives we have is a good collection. Does it really comprise all the important stages in the evolution of railway locomotives and the activity of British engineering in constructing them or does it reflect merely those locomotives which happened to be available, happened to be cheap or appeared to be easy to rebuild in the first place and maintain subsequently? It may be recalled that the British Transport Commission was provided with a considered list of steam locomotives meriting preservation, drawn up by an expert advisory committee, but that later events stultified this rational procedure.

The question of selection thus presents itself at once, and will appear again.

Road vehicles

This group comprises such things as motor cars, motor cycles, bicycles, commercial vehicles, traction engines, etc. Private motor cars are the most illustrious part of this group and have received a great deal of attention. Without question the best display and the largest is at the Montagu Motor Museum in Hampshire. This museum has also collected examples of most other types of road vehicles. All over the country other museums, big and small, specialized and non-specialized, have examples of one sort or another in states varying from the immaculate to the shoddy. Private preservation is immensely important. Probably as many old road vehicles are privately owned as are in museums. Many of those in private ownership are in outstanding condition and they frequently survive long journeys because they are in significantly better shape now than they were when built.

Aviation

It would seem that further collection in this field is pretty well hopeless. Almost all that is available in the nature of historic aircraft must by now have been located and preserved. When the Royal Air Force was looking recently for a Hawker Hind light bomber, one had to be brought back from Afghanistan. This is a significant group, then, if only because it is one where preservation is complete. There are a number of aircraft collections in Great Britain either in existence or planned. A number of these preserved machines are still operational. In the *Journal of the Royal Aeronautical Society* for August 1959 lists were published indicating what a large collection of British and foreign aircraft exists in

Great Britain; 136 British aircraft and 51 foreign ones. A minority pre-date 1914 but the important point is the existence of a catalogue enabling an overall picture of the position to be gained.

Stationary prime movers

An alternative name might be engines. Every type is represented, some by several examples. There are very many internal combustion engines, either diesel or petrol, designed for such functions as pumping, generating electricity and driving other sorts of machinery. All manner of steam engines have been preserved (at least in small numbers) ranging from early beam engines to later horizontal engines and early steam turbines. Electric motors and generators are numerous and various sorts of gas engines appear in large museums. In a few places the types of engine mentioned are operational but the vast majority are not. With a few exceptions windmills and water-mills have survived up and down the country only as outdoor specimens—that is, they are in the class of immovable relics. But at least they have been preserved, in most cases, along with the machinery they were built to drive. The Wind and Watermill Section of the Society for the Preservation of Ancient Buildings has been particularly active here. The vast majority of movable engines, that is of those in museums, are now detached from the equipment which they once operated.

Machine tools

This short title is taken to designate a large group of contrivances for performing all sorts of functions. At one extreme it covers the genuine machine tools such as lathes, shapers, milling machines, gear cutters and so on. These constitute an important section because many are original pieces (perhaps the work of Maudslay and Whitworth) and represent one of Great Britain's most significant contributions to technology. Especially fascinating is a representative group of eight machines from the Portsmouth Block-making Machinery. This is of great significance as the first large-scale plant to use machine tools in a mass production process. Other examples of the equipment still survive in the block mills in Portsmouth and fortunately there is hope that they too may be preserved *in situ*. Many other pieces of machinery for performing a list of operations too lengthy to detail are preserved in one place or another. In the absence of a catalogue it is impossible to be specific about this category beyond recognizing it as one where a great deal has been saved.

Models

Historic models—those constructed in the period by the same craftsmen who made the full-size objects—are extremely valuable to the technological historian as a record when the full-size objects have vanished, and to the museum curator for their convenience of display and authenticity. Some models—especially ship models, of which hundreds have survived—were made to show the proposed design of the future ship; others record in faithful detail the proud craftsmanship of a particular firm making locomotives, traction-engines, and even production machines.

These authentic models, which are virtually equivalent in evidential value to the full-scale object, must of course be distinguished from modern reconstructions (either in the form of full-scale replicas or of scale models) which, however useful for display and instruction, have no independent historical validity (and are sometimes known to "improve" on the original design!).

Craft industries

There must be hundreds if not thousands of items connected with craft industries. They include the manufacturing side of such industries, that is, the tools and apparatus used to make things, as well as the products themselves. This category covers the museums of Great Britain generally and is not restricted to technological museums or those with departments of technology. Evidently this situation reflects the fact that craft technology is widely looked upon as typical of the country's life in general and is not viewed as being technological in some narrow sense. There is moreover the point, very important, that craft relics tend to be small and once acquired present much less of a problem in terms of space and upkeep. Thus it is inevitable that so much has been kept at the expense perhaps of bigger and heavier items.

An examination of those aspects of technology which have been well covered leads to an obvious question. Why is it that *these* are the ones which have been emphasized while others have been ignored? There are several answers.

In the first place sentiment plays an important rôle. Railway locomotives exert an almost magical power over enthusiasts and

laymen alike and it is this which accounts for the tremendous interest in railway relics. It would be rash to infer that railway locomotives are so important in the history of nineteenth-century engineering as the number preserved might suggest; clearly, however, the locomotive does occupy a special place in British engineering history.

To some extent the same sentiment applies to old motor cars and traction engines. Nothing is more fashionable, or more satisfying to people in their leisure, than to be engaged in the business of finding old motor cars, restoring them to immaculate condition and then showing them off.

In all aspects of the history of transport public interest is a vital factor. Restoration and preservation is an expensive business and it is simply good business to concentrate on projects and activities which the public will support with money. This is true for instance of restored railway lines, which are very popular, but it does not necessarily follow that these lines are truly representative of railway history. Similarly a collection of old motor cars is likely to be popular and lucrative. But it does not follow that such a collection is historically valuable simply because it exists.

The existence of a large number of models is easily explained. They represent an attractive and simple method of display either when the real thing is too big to handle or when no example has survived.

In the case of prime movers popularity again seems to account for the large number of preserved examples. The idea of producing mechanical power from basic fuels such as coal and oil has always intrigued people and in so far as "engines" are a basic technological concept it is no surprise that so many examples are in existence. Much the same is true of machine tools and machinery generally; these are, simply, *interesting*. Moreover, machinery constitutes a large proportion of the total engineering picture and it is inevitable therefore that much has survived.

If it is accepted that certain technological fields have been well covered and others not so well or not at all, then how good are the collections of the most popular type? The question is difficult to answer. The study of the history of technology is a comparatively new field of research and it will take time to establish anything approaching a complete view on which proper criteria can be based; criteria, that is, which will enable us to say that such and such an item is important while something else is not. However, it is inconceivable that every railway locomotive preserved is an important relic; only a few may be that and some of them may be the ones in the worst condition and not those on which most care has been lavished.

Yet even if there were sharp criteria by which the conservationist could separate the sheep from the goats, in order to form a complete, balanced collection in a perfect museum, this ideal could not be achieved. In the absence of a national catalogue it is impossible to look at the problem on a national scale and decide: "This kind of thing is well represented in our museums; that should be located, if possible, and preserved." One cannot, at present, discern the significant gaps that ought, if possible, to be filled. Collections have been composed by acquiring whatever was available of possible interest; and fortunately so. We can hardly, at this stage, be regretful if our national resources are as regards some manifestations of technology almost excessively rich; we only regret their poverty in other respects. Still, one cannot ignore the fact that sentiment, opportunism (in the best sense) and shortage of both space and money have been powerful forces in shaping our national collections in the history of technology as they exist today, and have caused the loss of many important historic items —important to the expert, at any rate. Among all our hundreds of steam locomotives, for example, there is only one example of the singular and important Beyer-Garratt designs to be seen in this country (on the Festiniog Railway), and this was recovered from Tasmania and is a very small example. Certainly the vast majority were built for export but of those which were at one time in use in Great Britain not a single one has survived.

Apart from topics just considered which have been very well covered, there are several where the situation appears to be adequate, which is not to say that more could not be done and probably will be through some of the projects currently afoot.

Textile technology

This was a very important factor in the Industrial Revolution, especially in the north of England. Thus in museums in places such as Blackburn, Bolton, Bradford, Halifax, Helmshore, Huddersfield and Leigh there are exhibits relating to textile production. Another group occurs in the Midlands at Coventry, Hartlebury,

Leicester and Nottingham and there are collections also in Scotland, Ulster and London. The principal emphasis is on the early textile machines such as the "spinning jenny", Arkwright's frame and Crompton's mule, presumably because these items, quite apart from their pioneering importance, are not very large and are relatively simple mechanically; however, some collections (for example, those at Leicester and Nottingham) do extend to the twentieth century. Future museums, if they come into existence, e.g. in Manchester, will add more textile displays and the hope is that they will include some of the larger and more fully mechanized devices of the nineteenth century. Many of the museums mentioned contain collections of finished textiles as well as the machines themselves; these are also represented in collections of historic costume, such as that of the Victoria and Albert Museum.

Mining

Great Britain had a long and important history of mining for coal and metals even before the nineteenth century when mining expanded greatly. In fact one of the first technological museums, that built up by Holman Brothers at Camborne in Cornwall, is devoted to local mining engineering. Other important museums are the Museum of the Department of Mining Engineering at the University of Newcastle-upon-Tyne, the Museum of Science and Engineering in the same city, Salford Science Museum and the Science Museum in London. All the items shown in museums have been moved from their original locations and any attempt to represent the overall structure of a mine resorts to models or diagrams. So far it is predominantly small relics which have been preserved. For the future there are plans to display larger items, such as the winding engine from Beamish colliery, and these will have to be dealt with either in open air museums or *in situ*. Derelict mines, both for coal and metals, abound and perhaps a few could be reopened to the public. This would be very expensive. However, the National Coal Board, which has already carried out some preservation and is more sympathetic than most nationalized industries, may be a useful ally here. It has already assisted the Salford Science Museum to set up a replica coal mine in 1958.

Metals

Mining metal ores belongs to the previous section. The extraction of metals from the ores and the subsequent working of them is dealt with in a number of museums. Again, generally small items only have been preserved, the apparatus of metal working and also a large range of products. Models and diagrams are commonly used. Exceptional amongst museums devoted to metallurgy is the old works at Abbeydale near Sheffield. Indeed this very fine exhibit has even been referred to as "the finest industrial museum in the country". Abbeydale industrial hamlet contains a crucible furnace, tilt forge, workshops, warehouses, counting house and workmen's cottages all grouped round a large courtyard near the River Sheaf. The dam and water-wheels are in working order. As might be expected, there is a good deal else of importance in the Sheffield area: for example, one of the very few surviving cementation furnaces; and it is to be hoped that the success of the Abbeydale venture will encourage more activity.

The other well-known iron-working centre is Coalbrookdale, centre of the Darbys' crucial developments. Allied Ironfounders have seen to the preservation of some of the original furnaces along with examples of the iron-casting techniques. There is a small museum covering the history of iron working including dozens of iron objects, in some cases made from the Coalbrookdale Company's original patterns.

The non-ferrous metals have received less attention; they are not of course as important as iron and steel. The Swansea Museum has material relating to aluminium and nickel and other museums contain examples of the equipment used in working lead, tin and copper especially, plus examples of products. The Steel Company of Wales' museum at Llanelli is devoted to the history of tin-plating. Derelict non-ferrous metal mines and workings can be found in Cornwall, Wales, Derbyshire and the Pennines; and the Zennor Folk Museum (near St Ives, Cornwall) contains a good collection of models relating to the local mining industry, tools, and other relics. Most deserted workings are beyond the point at which preservation is viable but one or two may yet be considered.

The history of metallurgy is unusual in that it has a historical society dealing exclusively with its interests, namely the Historical Metallurgy Group. The group exists principally for the purposes of research rather than preservation, but through its work an idea of what might be worth preserving has been gained.

WHAT SHOULD BE CONSERVED

Even the existence of a catalogue would not help to list specimens which do not exist. One must resort to a process of elimination. Bearing in mind which fields have been well covered it is then necessary to examine the history of technology as a whole to see what has been left out. The following topics appear to be the most significant but there may be others.

Shipbuilding and ships

By this is meant the full-size vessels and not models, which as mentioned already have been extensively collected. Size is basically the problem here. There is not, and never has been, a lack of interest in Great Britain in ships of every type. Certainly a few examples are preserved and the smaller they are, the more likely their survival. However, a very small ship constitutes a big museum exhibit. *Turbinia*, beautifully preserved in the Museum of Science and Engineering in Newcastle-upon-Tyne, is a very small vessel by shipbuilding standards but a very large thing for a museum to cope with. The *Cutty Sark*, now dry-docked at Greenwich, is rather bigger and in terms of preservation too large even to go indoors. *Victory*, like the *Constitution* at Boston, Massachusetts, is happily still with us. Less well-known is *Peggy*, a small, late nineteenth-century vessel preserved at Castletown, Isle of Man.

Even quite small ships of importance and interest have slipped through the net of the preservationist. Plans to maintain a nineteenth-century paddle steamer were never realized though the *Duke of Devonshire* was the subject of a great deal of attention and activity. At least two nineteenth-century paddle tugs are in theory still available but it seems most likely that only a few bits and pieces of one of them will be retained. The last Severn trow was recently broken up, Bristol Channel pilot cutters are becoming rare, no example of a Humber Keel is known but at least one Norfolk wherry is still operational. Sailable Thames barges have almost disappeared.

If this is the situation regarding small vessels, what chance is there of keeping a big one or even several? In a sense the problem is not serious because there are already very few Victorian ships worthy of any attention at all. Two are well known: S.S. *Great Britain*, now a hulk in the Falkland Islands, and H.M.S. *Warrior* whose corpse at present forms a part of an oil jetty in South Wales. There are plans to save both and both are significant specimens of shipbuilding. But money is a major problem because the cost of moving these vessels to new moorings, restoring them and subsequently maintaining them is likely to be enormous. In any case their engines, gear, furniture and equipment have largely disappeared.

Really big ships *can* be coped with however. The *Queen Mary* and *Queen Elizabeth* have found homes in the United States, but it is relevant to note here that both are intended to serve other functions apart from merely being preserved. The idea of using a preserved ship as a museum in itself appears to be a necessary part of the whole operation.

Agricultural technology

A few museums, none large, are devoted to this subject. The existing collections do not seem to do justice to the importance of agriculture in the national life and economy down to the 1870s in particular. During the nineteenth century agriculture was increasingly mechanized but precious little of this mechanization is visible in museums or collections. The basic problem here is simple. Agricultural technology is regarded as a mundane, even an irrelevant, aspect of technology—it has no engineering glamour—and it is almost entirely lacking in sentiment and romance. This raises a basic issue. Should preservation be directed to fields which are popular and entertaining or should collections be built up according to their fundamental importance? Agriculture is an extremely important business.

Electronics

As far as the importance of electronics is concerned the period 1815–1914 only covers pioneer work connected with radio. Very little has been preserved. Practically nothing has survived of Marconi's work in the Isle of Wight; his station at Poldhu on the Lizard is marked by a simple plaque. There are very few surviving examples of transmitting and receiving equipment and unfortunately it is now probably too late to rectify this situation. However, an argument in favour of the erection of a museum of radio history was recently advanced in *Industrial Archaeology* (Vol. 5, no. 1, p. 52). But if a comment about the post-1914 position can

3

be made, electronic engineering is a field that needs further attention. Where is the historic magnetron that was carried to the United States in 1942?

Civil engineering

Victorian civil engineering relics form an interesting category because so many are still in use and, in a great many important cases, the problem of preservation has hardly arisen.

In the late eighteenth century and the early part of the nineteenth Britain built up her network of canals which included fine examples of civil engineering works: embankments, locks, dams, bridges, tunnels and aqueducts. Now that canal transport has almost entirely disappeared many of these works have gone out of use but most still exist. Very often they are simply too large to move and as far as preservation is concerned they clearly fall into the category of immovable relics. The future use of our inland waterways for recreational purposes will, it is to be hoped, ensure the survival of such masterpieces as Telford's aqueduct at Pontcysyllte. But other items are in danger such as the aqueduct at Longdon-on-Tern and various canal tunnels, the one at Dudley for instance, built between 1778 and 1792, and lock-staircases at many places.

Some examples of civil engineering on the railways have already been lost, including the whole series of Brunel's timber viaducts in South Wales and the West Country. But where the railways still operate the engineering works are usually safe for the time being. The Royal Albert Bridge at Saltash in fact is to be strengthened for future use. Box Tunnel will be safe so long as the rail link between Paddington and Bristol is in use. Preservationists should have an eye on the future however. If an item such as the Forth Railway Bridge were ever to become redundant and was thought to be worthy of conservation, the problem would be an enormous one and much greater than anything faced so far. Many railway bridges over roads (as well as bridges carrying roads) have been modified or destroyed in the course of road widening.

It is in the nature of civil engineering that its works are built to serve for a long period and Victorian examples are especially typical of this. One is compelled to point out though that from an earlier period, the late eighteenth century, there is the tragic example of the Iron Bridge at Coalbrookdale which is in poor condition but is without doubt the most important civil engineering relic in Great Britain. It was not only the first iron bridge in the world but the first really big iron structure of any sort. Whereas an earlier French attempt at an iron bridge had been a failure, Abraham Darby the third, grandson of the pioneer of iron smelting from coal, succeeded brilliantly. The bridge is based on a set of five semicircular cast-iron ribs spanning 100 feet with a rise of 50 feet. Each half-rib was cast in one piece in open moulds, a major metallurgical feat for the time (1776). Three hundred and seventy-eight tons of iron were used in the construction, which was effected without nuts, bolts, rivets, screws or welds; all the members are held in position with dovetails and dowels as if the bridge was made of wood. The Iron Bridge is a unique monument and no one with whom the Survey made contact doubted that its preservation was a matter of the utmost urgency and top priority.

Chemical technology

This branch of technology is at a double disadvantage; its relics are large and they lack glamour. Whatever the historical importance of a Victorian gas works, it is not calculated to compete in appeal with old motor cars nor is it so convenient to manage. Chemical technology involves complicated processes and elaborate apparatus which are difficult for the uninitiated to comprehend. But the fact remains that chemical technology is a very important field and especially so in the Victorian period which really saw the birth of industrial chemistry. Material does survive which could be preserved. Fakenham Gas Works has been argued over for some time while at the moment of writing the so-called "Iron Duke", a machine used in the manufacture of rubber, has come on to the "preservation market" but a home for it cannot be found. It is very large, is apparently of no interest to most people but is, nevertheless, a unique and important relic of the industry it represents.

Recently attempts have been made at the Plastics Institute to interest members in a historical group. At one level there is a good deal of interest amongst members but it does not extend to the organization of an active body which could do something about preservation. In general this seems to be common within most industries, not just the chemical industry.

We may therefore expect that any historian of the future

interesting himself in the alkali industry based on the Leblanc process, the coal-gas industry, or the manufacture of rubber—all of these being industries of great importance to the economy of Victorian Britain, and largely of British invention and development —will be compelled to study their technologies in books and papers with only a little aid from models, photographs, and a few rare actual survivals. It may be doubted whether there is a lead-chamber (for making sulphuric acid) or a salt-cake kiln (for making soda) left anywhere in this country. Just as well, it may be said; the processes are long out of date, and these and others practised by the chemical manufacturers (whose heaped wastes still pollute the rivers of the Midlands and the North) contributed greatly to the worst social horrors of Victorian Britain. But they were part of that Britain, they were undoubtedly as historic as the dinosaur, and equally they have vanished.

Heavy engineering

This category comprises equipment used in industry for heavy work, such things as drop forges, power hammers, rolling mills, large machine tools used for manufacturing big components such as shafts and gears, presses and the like. These items in fact must be classed as movable because their preservation cannot be undertaken *in situ*. When they become redundant in a workshop they are replaced and the old piece of equipment goes outside to be cut up or, perhaps, to be taken to a museum. But such a museum faces a serious problem of transportation, space and strength. Heavy engineering equipment is difficult to move, requires considerable space for display and imposes prodigious loads on the floor of the museum building—the ground floor, no other could possibly cope. This category, for the reasons given, has been badly neglected.

Plans, documents and drawings

The question of preservation in this category came to a head recently when the British Transport Commission elected to sell some of its plans and drawings. Many knowledgeable people expressed the view, an entirely accurate one, that documentary relics are vital and, as mentioned earlier, are often able to yield information not to be derived from any other source. It is incontestable that far more documentary relics have been destroyed than ever have been saved. There are two reasons for this. When a firm or industry is modernizing or expanding, old papers are very easy to dispose of not only literally but also in the sense that consciences are seldom disturbed. But even when an attempt is made to offer collections to a museum or archive they frequently cannot be accepted. In the first place they are bulky and in the second place their technical character renders them more difficult for the ordinary archivist or librarian to deal with. Probably only a small proportion of the plans and drawings are worth permanent retention, nor would there be space for all; all must be sifted through, identified, and the permanent collection (ideally) properly indexed. The problem is to acquire the services of experts who can separate the important from the insignificant, confidently put the latter aside, and describe the remainder.

The sale of British Railways drawings further raises the question: where should collections of drawings and plans be housed when firms or organizations no longer wish (or are able) to retain them? Technical Museums are an obvious and desirable choice but the regional, county or city archives of Great Britain also offer possibilities. There can be no objection of principle to storing technical records in the relevant public archive office and in certain cases this is done automatically—in the case of Acts of Parliament relating to railways and canals, for instance. In practice, however, problems of space, time and expertise are critical. The County Record Office in Hertford, for instance, expressed the opinion that it could not possibly contemplate housing the technical records from de Havilland's even if they were available.

The Records Preservation Section of the British Records Association is concerned with the preservation of technical records, and the Association dealt specifically with this problem at its Annual Conference in 1966. However, it is relevant to note that they place technical records in the category which "should always be *considered* for preservation" and not the category which "should always be preserved". The National Register of Archives, part of the Historical Manuscripts Commission, sets out to record the location, content and availability of all collections of documents in England and Wales and this includes the records of industrial and commercial concerns. From time to time they publish lists on Sources of Business History which contain valuable information on technical records. The National Register does not itself keep any documents because its function is to provide an up-to-date guide to collections elsewhere. The Business Archives Council should be mentioned as well because they too are anxious to ensure that technical records are not lost. Moreover in 1966 the Business Archives Council arranged a showing of some old industrial films in the hope that this would bring more similar material to light. Films in fact constitute an important part of the preservation picture. It is highly desirable to gather together all the old films of technological interest which can be found, to persuade industries to make film records of places, processes and prime movers before they are demolished, and to establish centrally a fund to finance simple film records. One of the problems about films, however, is that they are bulky and require proper preservation in the National Film Archive. It must be stressed too that it is not enough merely to make a film of something without taking the necessary steps to have the negative preserved in optimum condition.

All the above organizations are central to the problem of organizing the preservation of technical records and providing the necessary reference tools even though their facilities for actually storing the relevant documents are limited.

Nevertheless, it seems that the problem of securing reasonable quantities of technological records (drawings, photographs, plans, accounts etc.) for the future is basically a financial one. In existing local archives the start of an organization for dealing with such material already exists, and indeed County Archivists have already shown initiative in looking after it. But extra costs obviously arise if an industrial archive reaches sizeable proportions. Again, it seems likely that the necessary talent could be assembled for processing the material, if money were available for the purpose. In any case, it is worth remembering that when firms move their premises, or go out of business, or simply decide to clear their files, local knowledge is nearly always the necessary pre-requisite to any action for preservation, and the action to be speedy and effective must often be local also.

Pottery and glass making

The most significant aspect of this group is the attention which has been given to products at the expense of the technological processes themselves. Hundreds of pottery specimens have been lovingly preserved but examples of the equipment used to make them are rare. In Stoke-on-Trent the Spode-Copeland Museum and the Wedgwood Museum have magnificent pottery collections but cannot be regarded as technical museums.

On the other hand the Pilkington Glass Museum in St Helens is generally considered to be a fine achievement and the best "company museum" to date. With the possible exception of the Corning Glass Museum* at Corning, New York, it has developed into the best record of glass-making technology in the world. Apart from the display of products and techniques the museum incorporates the old Ravenhead Glass Works where cast plateglass was first made in England in 1773.

In this section mention should be made of brick-making. As far as could be ascertained this industry, which continues to be very important, has not been "preserved" at all. Nor is anyone very sure what possibilities exist.

Leather trades

There are many preserved examples of boots and shoes in both public and private museums, such as that of Clarks of Street. The technology of manufacture, however, has not been well covered except, as might be imagined, in Northampton. Between them the Central Museum and Art Gallery and the College of Technology have collected some prize items but at present are not able to show them as well or completely as might be expected.

Leather work also appears in the form of the finished product in other fields, e.g. upholstery, but the processes and equipment involved seem not to have attracted much attention. Furniture manufacture in particular and carpentry in general appear to be regarded as being on the fringe of the main stream of nineteenth-century technology; it was after all the century of iron and steel.

Printing and paper making

Printing presses are numerous but they occur in isolation in various museums, non-technical just as much as technical. The Science Museum has the most complete collection of relics depicting the development of nineteenth-century printing technology. The printing industry itself is interested in the history of the trade through the St Bride Institute and the Printing Historical Society,

* There is an interesting critique of this Museum in *Technology and Culture*, Vol. 10 (1969), pp. 68–83, the second of such "exhibit reviews" to be published in this journal.

but no plans for preservation of machines and equipment have materialized.

The British Board and Papermakers Association has been instrumental in collecting material relating to the techniques of paper making in the now disused paper-mill at St Mary Cray in Kent. Financial restrictions, however, have prevented the establishment of a National Paper Museum but at least the collection has been retained in storage. It is to be hoped that the museum will one day be built and that the items will not be dispersed in the meantime.

There are a number of basic factors accounting for the fact that some aspects of the history of technology or certain departments of a technological museum prove popular, while others have been neglected. Some are relatively modern technologies and consequently are not revered in the same way as the technologies of the high years of the Industrial Revolution. Size is the fundamental problem in the case of shipbuilding, heavy engineering and certain aspects of chemical engineering. The plant associated with gas making and steel manufacture is large; too large to move and very expensive to preserve *in situ* even if there were sufficient interest in preservation in the first place. In the case of much Victorian civil engineering the preservation problem has not yet arisen.

AGENCIES AND PROCEDURES

Many varied procedures are in use in order on the one hand to discover what rare pieces of Victorian (or earlier) technological equipment may be acquired for a museum or private collection, or on the other to discover what possibly meritorious items or installations are in danger of destruction. (It will be appreciated that these twin processes are not quite identical; one can think of machines and other objects which many museum curators would welcome with open arms; on the other hand, in the case of less beguiling objects the difficulties in the way of preservation may easily prevail.) Further, preservation or conservation may be secured in a number of ways. These procedures and ways are commonly informal, but not the less effective for that. They depend on the individual's having a close knowledge of, and many friends in, a particular area or an individual industry. They depend greatly on the energy and repute of the individual museum curator or collector.

In general, the position is confused. Notably, in the private sector, though there is widespread enthusiasm for "industrial archaeology" and the recording at least or if possible conservation of the heritage from nineteenth-century industry, there is virtually no co-ordination or co-operation among the countless individuals and small groups concerned. There is no clear universal objective and certainly no widely accepted plan for technological conservation. Activities tend to be local, piecemeal, and sometimes one-sided.

At the official level the Ministry of Public Building and Works has the power to schedule industrial monuments for preservation and attend to the work involved in their restoration and maintenance. Unfortunately there is considerable difficulty in defining an Industrial Monument. It does not fall neatly into the two existing categories of Ancient Monuments and Historic Buildings and traditionally these have commanded attention and money for upkeep. However, in 1967 the Ministry prepared a memorandum on the scheduling of industrial monuments, the important part of which was published in *Industrial Archaeology* (Vol. 4, no. 2, pp. 170–71). The memorandum brought out the problem of deciding to what extent machinery, equipment and fittings were a proper part of an industrial monument, although it was affirmed that industrial monuments themselves were entirely valid items for consideration by the Ministry. Items such as windmills and canal locks were regarded as structures, with their mechanical equipment included in the specification. So too were beam engines since with them the engine house—a structure—is an integral part of the machine. But the difficulties remain. A bridge is so obviously a permanent structure that it clearly qualifies as an industrial monument. If on the other hand the machinery in an industrial monument could conceivably be removed to a museum then the Ministry of Public Building and Works would not be likely to schedule it even though they might be persuaded to consider such a proposal. Unfortunately, though it may be technically feasible to remove machinery to a museum, it may be very undesirable to do so on the grounds that the building and its machinery would be far less significant when separated. A water-mill for instance might be scheduled on the grounds that the building plus its wheel was a genuinely fixed structure, properly qualifying as an industrial monument. But what of the other mechanical equipment of the mill, all the ancillary fittings and machinery which in principle could go to a museum with the result that the "industrial monument" would be a mere skeleton? The building and wheel robbed of all the bits and pieces which were once part and parcel of the mill's work can hardly be regarded as proper preservation.

It will be noticed as a corollary of the Ministry's decision to protect machinery as part of an industrial monument, that the decision still leaves absolutely unprotected any machinery, however important, if the building housing it is *not* to be maintained as an industrial monument.

The Ministry of Housing and Local Government is empowered to "list" buildings or monuments of importance, but experience suggests that only those placed in Grade 1 of the list are likely to enjoy even a slight safeguard.

If the legal means to protect industrial monuments is unsatisfactory then the position regarding all other technical relics is worse. There is *no* means to protect them at all, no official method by which any interested party can require the owner of an old machine, machine tool, motor car or any other vehicle, camera, radio set or anything, to look after the item and offer it to a museum when the owner no longer has an interest in it or use for it. Individuals, firms and local authorities can and do demolish and dispose of things without being answerable to any body or authority. These acts are not necessarily wilful acts of destruction or awkwardness. If the significance and interest of a technological relic is not appreciated by the owner he can hardly be blamed for disposing of it. The problem arises when a collector or museum curator has located a specimen, made out a case for its preservation but still cannot guarantee its being secured. Money comes into the picture. Many old machines, especially big ones, can command high scrap prices which the owner is not anxious to forfeit. A museum must at least equal the scrap value in order to acquire the object. It must also find the money to carry it away since the owner cannot be expected to pay for the cost of transport.

Despite the woefully inadequate means to give legal protection to technological relics, many do nevertheless find their way into safe keeping. All sorts of approaches and methods are currently in use.

The location of industrial monuments is generally not difficult. Many because of their size and importance are well known throughout the country and have been for years, even decades. Indeed the importance and widespread fame of certain specimens perhaps act against their interests. Those who wish to protect and preserve them may become complacent through believing that a certain bridge or aqueduct is such a conspicuously well-known component of history that neglect or demolition could never happen—no one could ever be so stupid not to realize how valuable the item is. Unfortunately this is not always true. In the case of less well known outdoor relics the vast band of industrial archaeologists at present combing the country is rapidly locating new things and the National Record of Industrial Monuments is designed to accumulate this information and make it available for reference and for action. There is not now a shortage of industrial monuments to be preserved. The shortage is of money to carry out the work.

Once an industrial monument has been located and selected as suitable for preservation various things can happen. The Ministry of Public Building and Works may take action if the item fits their definition and they have the necessary funds. Otherwise private individuals or groups must do what they can and often this involves making an approach to the owner of the building, if there is an owner. (In the case of derelict mills and mines and the like this is not the case.) The outcome of negotiations of this sort is entirely unpredictable because in most cases no one is actually obliged to do anything. Results depend on the initiative, energy and tact of the preservationists, the available finances and equipment and the attitudes, commitments and sympathies of owners, local authorities and industrial organizations.

Assuming that the monument can be acquired and restored, the next problem is to find the money for its upkeep—not just maintaining the fabric and machinery but also providing access and keeping would-be vandals at bay. In a few cases this work is done by the Ministry of Public Building and Works. Sometimes local authorities take charge but this arrangement is not always satisfactory because political issues can influence the status of industrial monuments. The Historic Buildings Council has helped to preserve such things as windmills and aqueducts and the same is true for the National Trust; however, in the latter case action can only be taken if a large capital endowment is forthcoming. Perhaps the best solution is a preservation trust provided its independence and autonomy can be guaranteed. Two examples of the preservation of industrial monuments by means of private trusts are set out in

Appendix III. Examples of preservation by industry itself are rare but Allied Iron Founders (the Darbys' furnace at Coalbrookdale), Bristol Waterworks (two beam engines at Blagdon) and Associated Lead (Elswick shot towers) are examples. Unfortunately at the end of 1968 and in spite of Associated Lead's good intentions, the Elswick shot towers were pronounced unsafe and had to be taken down.

In the case of "indoor" relics, which almost always means movable items, the procedures for locating specimens are anything but organized. Basically, two parties are involved: museums and preservationists on the one hand, who want to locate items, and industrial firms on the other hand, who are the owners of the equipment. Often suitable relics for preservation turn up by chance. They might be noticed by a historian conducting his research, by someone else who mentions their existence to a historian or museum curator or industrial archaeologist, or perhaps by a person from within industry itself such as an insurance inspector or a workman. In some instances determined individuals decide in advance that such and such a specimen might be possible to locate and then set about finding it using all sorts of detection methods. If they are successful they must then persuade the owners to part with it at some future date. The Birmingham Museum of Science and Industry takes the trouble to affix small plates to movable specimens while they are still in their private owner's possession as a reminder that the item is of interest.

Alternatively, historically conscious firms sometimes offer specimens to museums if they think they have items of interest. It is encouraging that this should be done. However, existing museums are desperately short of space and good-tempered negotiation is necessary to ensure that a worthwhile object finds a proper home. No one concerned for technological conservation wishes to discourage industry's own eagerness to conserve what is no longer productively useful, and it would facilitate the task of conservation, obviously, if museums were less desperately pressed for space and money.

Preservation of movable objects is very much a game of chance: the chance that something might be found and the chance that something might be offered. Pervading the whole field is a sort of grapevine which is built up in any region over a long period. It has to be cultivated by the interested parties and in some cases is very effective. It is also very delicate. If a museum curator dies or moves to another place, his contacts may not be easily picked up by his successor. Even when they are, much time is lost and the natural sequence of events sharply interrupted.

In no sense is there a formal method of preservation for movable technical relics.

CURRENT PROJECTS

Already a great deal of technical conservation has been effected successfully. Even though existing collections are not perfectly balanced—since even in the best represented aspects of technology not all objects are of first-class importance, while major gaps also remain—we must be thankful for the considerable achievement so far, most of which can never be duplicated.

The large number of existing collections, ranging from the large to the very small, has not prevented the preparation of plans for new technical museums or departments of technology in existing museums. These plans are part and parcel of the tremendous surge of interest over the last decade in industrial archaeology. Various sentiments motivate industrial archaeologists and not all are serious students of technical history, but the effects of the movement are nevertheless beneficial. What is more, industrial archaeologists are responsible for more than just the climate in which preservation can flourish. In the first place it is their efforts which have often brought to light many industrial monuments and other relics which otherwise would probably have passed away unnoticed and unknown. Also, their time, effort and even money helps considerably in the location, recording, renovation and sometimes preservation of technological relics. For the future it is quite evident that their enthusiastic assistance will be of great value and more often than not essential.

Birmingham

There were plans for a complete re-development of the Museum of Science and Industry in Birmingham which led to the demolition of a good deal of the old museum, many items being put, temporarily it was believed, into store. The economic situation has forced this project to be shelved with the result that the museum is unable to show anything like all of one of the best collections in the country.

Bristol

Bristol City Museum has set up a department of technology and so far has collected a considerable range of items typical of the industrial history of Bristol and its surroundings. They have such things as a colliery winding engine from the North Somerset coalfield, some rope-making machinery, a number of steam and internal combustion engines made in the region, ship models, locomotives, horse-drawn road vehicles, aircraft and marine engines and the prototype "Bristol" lorry of the early 1950s. But very few items are yet exhibited, those that are comprising mainly ship models and carriages. The remainder is at present in store, in very cramped conditions, being renovated and rebuilt. This work is being done by one man and is a lengthy and difficult operation. Ultimately the aim is to exhibit the technological collection in a completely new city museum which, it is hoped, will be constructed in the centre of Bristol. But this is not likely to be soon. The position in Bristol also typifies another aspect of the problem of creating a museum of technology. Mr Neil Cossons, who has been so active in building up the nucleus of Bristol's technical collection, has been appointed to a new post in another city. It remains to be seen if he can be effectively replaced so as to ensure that his valuable work bears fruit.

Leicester

In Leicester plans for a technological museum are well advanced. The aim is to develop a disused pumping station, together with its four surviving beam engines, and the surrounding grounds. This riverside site about two miles from the centre of Leicester is very suitable for a technical museum of some size and the initial capital required, about £70,000, is not regarded as particularly high for such a project. The money has to be found, however, and future extensions will depend on the availability of yet more finance. Some of the collection is already on display, including a unique group of hosiery and knitting machinery at present in the Newarke Houses Museum. In the old Stoneygate tram terminus there is part of the transport collection including four railway locomotives and a selection from Mr S. W. A. Newton's photographic record of the construction of the Great Central Railway, and a road transport museum has now been opened in Oxford Street. In its final form the Museum of Technology for the East Midlands will comprise a

"Hall of Power" plus sections devoted to transport, founding and heavy engineering, mining and quarrying, hosiery and knitting, boots and shoes, and printing. In the case of this museum, the City of Leicester has promised to provide half the initial capital cost.

Manchester

In Manchester a start has been made towards the establishment of a museum of local science and technology. Collection of specimens has been going on for some time and, pending the construction of a brand-new and large museum building, a sample is now on view in the former Oddfellows' Hall. The life of this building is limited, however, and the crucial problem in Manchester is to find the money to build a new structure as soon as possible so that what should be a very fine collection can be properly housed.

In the final version of the museum it is intended to illustrate the history of the steam engine with a number of large specimens. Because of their size and the expense of moving them about they will not appear in the Oddfellows' Hall and instead models will be used for the time being. Other items scheduled to appear in the permanent museum include the products of Crossley Brothers, pioneer gas engine manufacturers, early Royce engines from the pre-Rolls Royce era, a recent jet engine and electrical power plant including some early Ferranti products. Other items include spinning and weaving machinery, some machine tools by Whitworth and a fascinating array of old cameras and other photographic material.

A significant aspect of the Manchester venture is the fact that the University of Manchester, the University of Manchester Institute of Science and Technology and Manchester City Council are agreed that the project should be a joint effort and all are in favour of the scheme. In order to raise nearly £2 million, the estimated capital cost for the new museum, their combined efforts will certainly be needed.

Coventry

In Coventry a very large collection consisting mainly of transport relics, cars and bicycles has been assembled. Unfortunately it is only possible to display a small selection from it in the Herbert Art Gallery, the remainder being stored in an old factory building.

Bradford

Bradford has collected together relics of textile machinery for possible display in the wool exchange.

Dudley

The County Borough of Dudley has plans for an Industrial Museum covering the history of the Black Country. The plan here is to emphasize industries which are not already dealt with in other West Midlands museums. At present work is being devoted to gathering together possible exhibits before it is too late. The next stage will be the acquisition of a suitable site on which to exhibit the museum collections, much of which can be shown in the open air. Finance is once again a key factor.

Another scheme in Dudley, which is of great interest, is the possibility of preserving and using that part of the Dudley Canal Line No. 1 which links the old Birmingham–Wolverhampton canal at Tipton to the Dudley Canal Line No. 2 at Park Head. The total length of canal to be preserved is $2\frac{1}{4}$ miles including 3,172 yards of tunnel in the middle of Dudley. This is now the longest accessible canal tunnel in the country and dates from the period 1778–92. If the canal and its tunnel can be restored to use it will be a fine addition to the overall picture of Britain's canal history.

North-east England

There are plans for other outdoor museums and easily the most impressive project is in the North-East. The idea is to create a vast open air museum showing the history of life in the area; industrial life will be a major part of the scheme. The amount of material already collected and put into store is no less impressive than the size of some of the exhibits such as the coal drop from Seaham Harbour and the Beamish colliery winding engine. The Northern Region Open Air Museum represents preservation on a grand scale and when realized will be very impressive. There is already great enthusiasm for the scheme but it will not be possible to complete the work either cheaply or quickly.

An important aspect of the project so far is the careful and absolutely necessary attention which has been given to the establishment of temporary storage space. An old army camp at Brancepeth is at present sheltering all manner of the smaller items including a host of agricultural machines and implements, complete shops such as a printer's, chemist's, photographer's and grocer's and relics of chain-making and mining. At Consett Iron Works are numerous transport relics including a selection of old trams, still operational, and destined to be run in the museum when it is finished. If there were not the means to store such a vast collection of relics they would certainly be lost for ever. Their final home could never be ready in time to house them straight away.

The organizers of the Northern Region Open Air Museum are also fully aware of the rôle which the public must play in such a venture. The public's support is not only vital in the early stages of planning but even more so when the museum is functioning. It must be both attractive and interesting if sufficient visitors are to be encouraged to part with their money. At the same time, though, it is believed that an open air technological museum is precisely the sort of display to which people will flock, especially if it covers the history of their own area.

Lea Valley

Recently the Greater London Council announced its plans to develop the Lea Valley as a huge recreational area at an immense cost. The creation of a technical museum is part of the project and coincidentally there are similarities to the Leicester scheme. Once more an old Victorian pumping station is to be used and beam engines will figure in the display although this time they will have to be moved. The Lea Valley project presents enormous possibilities for the future of preservation in the London area because of the scale on which the Lea Valley scheme has been conceived and the amount of money which promises to be available.

Ironbridge

The most recently announced project is for another open air museum, this time at Ironbridge. Probably no place in Great Britain is better placed for such an idea and none has a better claim. Here after all was the place where Abraham Darby first smelted iron with coke and set in motion a whole series of developments, many of which took place in the Ironbridge area at the instigation of the Darby family and their associates.

The museum will occupy two large sites, one at Coalbrookdale and the other at Coalport. The first site will embrace the existing

4

Coalbrookdale Company's museum which contains Darby's original furnace, an old dam, an eighteenth-century warehouse and various railway items. The second site, which has to be carved out of a hillside, will feature early blast furnaces, a pair of engine houses, an industrial tramway bridge and a canal section with a set of locks, the rebuilt Coalport canal incline and Telford's cast-iron aqueduct which will have to be moved from Longdon-upon-Tern. There are other items to be preserved as well. These include the former Coalport China Works, the famous Bedlam furnaces and four bridges: the Iron Bridge itself, the Coalport Bridge of 1818, the Albert Edward Railway Bridge and the "free" bridge, built in 1909, and one of the earliest examples of a reinforced concrete structure.

The Ironbridge Gorge Museum is an exciting prospect and a vast undertaking as well. There is little wonder that the Trust which has been formed to bring it about has launched an initial appeal for £1 million. The project is to be carried out as an integral part of the development of Telford New Town, the idea being that the new town will never obscure or lose contact with the history of the region it is designed to revitalize.

The projects for new technical museums outlined above coupled with already existing establishments indicate that there is no lack of preservation facilities in Great Britain. The means to preserve relics certainly exist and there are many knowledgeable and enthusiastic people involved in the process of finding relics and then attempting to restore and display them. What handicaps them above all else is lack of capital. Given the money, many people are poised to achieve a great deal.

In Appendix IV will be found a list of the more important projects for new museums together with the addresses of the people responsible.

CONCLUSIONS AND RECOMMENDATIONS

The conclusions and recommendations of this Report may be best approached by first reviewing a number of issues:

1. *Organization*

At present methods of conserving industrial buildings and technological equipment are haphazard and unco-ordinated, except in so far as these fall in the sphere of interest of such national institutions as the Ministry of Public Building and Works (see under *Agencies and Procedures*, above), the Science Museum or the National Maritime Museum.

Even the policy with regard to the vestiges of its own historical past of such a powerful and national body as British Rail seems curiously vacillating and open to criticism.

Regional and private conservation endeavours are, partly by choice, partly by necessity, partial and capricious in the way they operate to choose what shall be preserved and what lost to posterity. There are few or no standards of importance, and no measures to ensure that there is neither duplication nor failure to preserve something unique.

However, regionalism, the specificity of certain museums' rôles and the increasing scarcity (or expense) of the most popular subjects for technical conservation do operate in the opposite direction, mitigating the tendency to repeat the same kind of collection many times.

Moreover, though the results of personal enthusiasm may well be unbalanced, they have been of great value upon the national conservation scene (for example, with regard to scientific instruments, photographic apparatus, early steam engines and windmills). Any form of national programme that stultified private and regional efforts would, in our view, harm rather than advance the cause of technological conservation.

Any improvement of the "sieve" to ensure that worthwhile historical relics of Victorian (and later) technology are not lost through ignorance, inertia, poverty or lack of space will be worth while. The time available is short for conserving anything more of our great industrial past, and the responsibility falls wholly on ourselves for determining whether—of what remains unprotected—little or much, rationally or haphazardly selected, will be preserved for the future.

A National Plan of Action, based on a National Catalogue of what is already safely conserved, is put out of question by reasons of time and money, and might only yield bureaucratic pomposity. But it seemed to us that the organization of all who think rightly in this matter might be improved as follows:

A. At the most private level, a national organization for promoting the study of industrial archaeology might be formed, publishing a newsletter—or some such vehicle for co-ordination, rationalization and education. Dr R. A. Buchanan of Bath and others have this object very much at heart.*

B. At the museum level, it should be possible to improve communication and co-operation between those engaged in managing established museums or creating new ones, with a view to reducing duplication and competition. There is sometimes a professional rivalry between curators, as well as a reluctance to limit ambitions, and neither of these necessarily assist conservation in general. Could an existing body, the Museums Association, take a particular interest in the new technological museums? A single individual somewhere could at least act as a link and clearing-house of information, to whom appeal for help might be made in difficult cases.

C. The links between industrial archaeologists, some museums and the existing system of Record Offices might well be made closer and more friendly. Per cubic foot, documentary material is likely to prove more illuminating to historians of the future than hardware, and perhaps in some cases is all we can hope to preserve for a remote posterity. (Problems of the durability of modern paper and film suggest themselves here, but they are not peculiar to technological conservation.)

D. The legal protection of both industrial buildings (with or without technical equipment) and of equipment or machines, together with documentary material, independent of the building containing them, should be examined afresh. Despite recent strengthening of the law, many keen conservationists still feel that historic buildings or structures are too vulnerable to cupidity or neglect; machines and documents are far worse off. No one wishes to propose the creation of yet another governmental machine, but it would be worth while to review the whole position thoroughly, with legal advice.

One obvious private encouragement to conservation would be the existence of a fund which, through the agency of museums or private bodies, would make available the relatively small sums required to match the scrap-value of most machines and remove them to a museum or safe store. This would not be difficult to administer, for example through the NRIM.

---

* On the "Centre for the Study of the History of Technology" at Bath University, see *Technology and Culture*, Vol. 9 (1968), pp. 430–35.

Whether there should also be a legal control of the export of rare and valuable objects of technological interest we have not thought it necessary to consider.

2. Regionalism

We have been impressed by the depth and sincerity of interest in technological conservation outside London, and the several attempts to create regional foci at Bristol, Leicester, Manchester, Barnard Castle and elsewhere. It is virtually certain that at least four new provincial museums of technology will, in time, come into existence in some way or other. The only issue is: how much work of conservation will they be enabled to carry out?

The main centres of technological activity in Victorian Britain were, as everyone knows, outside London. The modern return of population and economic vigour to the south-east of the island is a direct reversal of the movement occasioned by the Industrial Revolution. The technological development of textile manufacture, metallurgical industry, chemicals, pottery and glass, shipbuilding and so on took place on Clydebank, Teesside, South Wales, the Black Country and the Potteries, Lancashire, the Midlands and the West Riding of Yorkshire. In these regions and nowhere else are both the monuments and the machines that created the wealth of Victorian England to be found—so far as they still exist outside museums. It seems not unreasonable to argue that regional museums offer the best opportunities for a display of regional technological history.

And it is trivially obvious that most bridges, mills, mines, warehouses, furnaces, cranes, tunnels, dams and so on must either be preserved where they were once useful, or crumble and be lost.

Therefore the link between industrial conservation and the provinces seems to us inescapable. In fact in sheer human terms the job cannot be done without the enthusiasm of the people on the spot.

3. Publicity

Despite the well-meaning efforts of the BBC at late evening hours, the case for preserving technological history has not been well made on a national scale. Too often preservation is regarded only as an interesting pastime for devoted amateurs. It could and should be much more. Professor Simmons has emphasized in his introductory statement that engineering is one of Great Britain's finest historical achievements and is unrivalled by any other nation. Rex Wailes has written that "This country led the way in industrial development and in many cases it is here, and only here, that the full range of that development can be seen." Quite apart from the sheer satisfaction of looking after our national heritage, it is nothing less than our responsibility to preserve a view of the country's technical history for the interest of posterity. Great Britain could have easily the finest set of technical museums in the world, with which no other country could possibly compete because no other possesses the material.

It is extraordinary how little impact the above facts have made. There needs to be conviction throughout the country that Great Britain's technical and industrial history is worthy of the interest and admiration not just of historians of technology and industrial archaeologists but the nation as a whole. If this point can be put across it should help to clear away many existing obstacles: lack of concern on the part of national and local authorities, ignorance in industry as to the possible value of old plant and equipment, and lack of financial assistance. Some die-hards and antagonists will doubtless remain unconvinced for the reasons that they hold now, but the benefits to be obtained from publicity will be considerable for the investment involved.

4. *Finance*

This is the crux of the whole issue. No one is in any doubt that lack of money is the main handicap to preservation. It prevents or at least hinders the establishment of new technological museums and departments of technology in existing museums. Moreover it is the vital factor in saving such industrial monuments as the Iron Bridge, whose threatened collapse would be a tragedy not to say a national scandal, and in arranging the preservation of large relics such as S.S. *Great Britain* or H.M.S. *Warrior*. In all these cases any number of people are ready and willing to take action; they have numerous plans of campaign, access to suitable material and promises of assistance, very often at no expense.

Money has to be spent in various ways. In the first place there is the "price" of the object itself. Many are offered free of charge but in those cases where the scrap price is required, or some other market value is quoted, then it has to be paid. Owners of relics have a right to demand a fair return on items they are prepared to part with. Immovable objects, generally big objects, must then be restored and if necessary and possible put into original condition and working order. Labour for such work is often free but skilled personnel where required and materials have to be paid for. Subsequently upkeep, access and protection from vandals adds to the bill annually. A typical figure cannot be quoted because the variation is considerable. Moreover preliminary quotations are unreliable because nearly all immovable historic objects are "one-off" jobs.

Once a movable piece of equipment has been acquired, the first financial problem is that of the cost of moving it. This depends on size and distance. The cost of dismantling the object and reassembling it in its new home (to which in turn reinforcements or alterations may be necessary) must also be taken into account.

Finally there is the cost of maintaining museums, or those parts of them in which technological history is represented, which will be augmented as fresh technological material is brought in: both capital costs for building, and regular running costs. (Again, it may be that in the case of new, regional museums the recurrent cost could be met in whole or part by charging an entrance fee; we have not thought fit to pursue this point, beyond remarking that pay-museums appear to succeed in other countries, and that the Montagu Motor Museum is a very successful and popular example in England.)

Even though everything neither can nor will be placed in a large, warmed building it is clear that the total cost of a great national effort to improve the conservation of our historic rôle in the growth of modern technology would be very great. A considerable capital development for the provision of buildings, roads, display-parks and car parks, public facilities and so forth would be required, and the recurrent costs of administering, guarding and maintaining both monuments and equipment could soon be built up to hundreds of thousands of pounds per year. Moreover, the contribution of volunteer labour (at present considerable outside national and public museums) must be expected to diminish in the future. Obviously it is impossible at this stage to prepare a financial forecast of what a major national effort would entail. However, in order to record some speculative estimates, it is our opinion that expenditures (at present prices) of the order of £20,000 per annum on minor non-recurrent grants for technological conservation, e.g. moving large machines to a store, and £10,000 per annum to each of two, three or four regional centres of activity, these being centres which are already actively engaged in preservation work and different centres being chosen each year, would at once have a very great effect indeed; they would enable much to be saved that will otherwise be lost, and new museums to be opened in the near future.

5. *Temporary storage*

The last section was concerned with permanent arrangements. But another crucial issue at the present time is that of temporary storage. Even if the funds were at hand (and they are not) new technological museums could not be erected overnight. As already remarked of the "Iron Duke", virtually every day equipment must be removed to a suitable, safe store or it will be taken away by a scrap merchant. Industrial firms will not and cannot give space to unwanted machinery for months and years; those who wish to conserve machinery must be prepared to have it thrust on their hands (literally!) at almost a moment's notice. At the present moment the establishment of a group of receiving depots scattered about the country, where materials may if necessary remain for long periods, is essential to the success of an extensive programme of conservation.

It is difficult to estimate the cost of storage. There are empty warehouses and mills in some places, but it must be emphasized that vandalism is always a problem. Any store must be secure, dry and guarded. It has been suggested that suitable buildings, under guard, might be found in the Royal Dockyards.

WHAT NEEDS TO BE DONE

Reviewing the whole question generally, it seemed to us that there were three chief types of possible activity:

A. The protection and maintenance of immovable industrial monuments—many examples are recorded in Appendix I—together with their equipment and machinery (if any) and the arrangement of the site in such a way as to permit the public to visit it.

B. The support by publicity, advice, and financial aid of regional and local museums, conservation societies, and county or regional archives, in so far as these are devoted to technology and industry. This form of support would chiefly aid the preservation of movable objects (machines, vehicles and so on), documents, photographs and films.

C. The establishment of a new Museum of Victorian Technology in London or elsewhere.

If a new National Museum were to be considered, it would be necessary to decide whether its function was mainly conservation or mainly educational display. While not wishing to deprecate the importance of the latter (depending on the use of photographs, dioramas, reconstructions, models and so on) it is obvious that a very fine educational exhibition may actually *conserve* nothing authentic. Hence, in so far as a new National Museum might be directed towards educating the public towards understanding Britain's technological achievement in history, it might move away from the conservation function.

It is our belief that Objectives A and B are to an overwhelming degree concerned with conservation, while at the same time properly making allowance for the interest and education of the public.

Next, the question must be considered: is there material suitable for conservation on such a scale as to justify a major effort? In Appendix I Dr R. A. Buchanan has reviewed the problems of conservation in a single region. It is quite certain (to consider Objective A first) that there are a very large number of immovable industrial monuments, from the Iron Bridge onwards, that are worthy of preservation, some of which are now or soon will be in danger of destruction because their usefulness is diminishing to zero. Present procedures and present financial resources are utterly unable to preserve them.

Everyone having any familiarity with "industrial archaeology" can detail instances; recently, for example, Mr Rex Wailes and others have discovered that the remarkable Gothic pumping-station at Papplewick in Nottinghamshire is in danger of destruction. Efforts to ensure its preservation are being made.*

As was stressed previously, not every nineteenth-century British industry can be represented by even one permanent monument. The shipyards of the past have gone for ever. And the same is true (Objective B) of museums containing transportable objects; prob-

---

* It has been estimated that the cost of operating the station for display on two days at weekends would be about £200 for each occasion.

ably in some respects the collections already housed in existing museums cannot be much extended. But again there is every reason to suppose that good museum material of many different kinds is still available and indeed is clamouring for museum space. So far as we could learn none of the new museum schemes suffers from lack of good exhibits—even though *some* kinds of exhibits are unprocurable. There is thus every reason to believe that the pursuit of Objectives A and B would lead to worthwhile results, though (as already remarked) it would be vain to think of duplicating either the Science Museum or the National Maritime Museum.

It will be obvious that the rôle and structure of a regional museum are properly distinct from those of a national museum.

We also wish to emphasize strongly the importance of a technological museum's not containing merely lifeless, inoperative machines. Many, if not all exhibits, should be capable of performing their original functions. Where there are steam-engines, for example, it should be possible, if only infrequently, to raise steam so that visitors can hear, see, and smell what a going steam-engine was like. We also believe that it is highly desirable in such a museum to display at least a few simple handicraft operations: wood-turning, for example, throwing a pot on a wheel, perhaps simple iron-working. And the products of such workshops should be available for purchase. The opportunity to see a craftsman at work is today at least as rarely available as the opportunity to inspect the splendid products and machines of Victorian technology.

PRIORITIES

It is our recommendation that, for any national conservation programme, the proper order of priorities in action would be as follows:

1. To take steps to encourage the proper processing and preservation of the documentary material concerning the history of technology and industry.
2. To organize as rapidly as possible a system of stores in which material may be held.
3. To support by grants from time to time museums, archives and conservation societies.
4. To protect and conserve immovable industrial monuments, in order that they may be visited.

5. To consider the establishment of a new National Museum of Technological History.

An explanation of this choice of priorities seems proper:

1. This is the easiest step to take, and one demanding only fairly small sums of money to inaugurate. Moreover, without documentation the physical remains will be unintelligible in the future.
2. Again, if this is not done much of the point of every other step may be lost; and the matter is rather one of organization than of finance.
3. This, in fact, goes hand in hand with the first two priorities. However, we do not believe that *by itself* the conferring of greater financial resources upon those who wish to create new technological museums would immediately solve all problems of conservation.
4. Protection of buildings and monuments is partly covered by the three first priorities; to some extent also this is a longer-term problem. And legislation is already in being, if not effective.
5. Demands fuller discussion in the light of the circumstances in which the Victorian Technology Survey came into being. It is our belief that a large historical movement should not be undertaken in order to provide employment for a particular building.

The arguments against concentrating a national conservation effort, as a first priority, on the establishment of a new National Museum in London are:

(a) the fact that the important centres of British technology were outside London, and so are their industrial monuments (this argument does not apply, obviously, to London's docks, railway stations, bridges and so on);
(b) the fact that the movement for technological conservation, and the projects for new museums, have their strengths outside London;
(c) the fact that London already has the Science Museum, the National Maritime Museum, and (it is hoped) a museum as a feature of the Lea Valley Scheme (see *Current Projects*).

The arguments in favour are:

(d) a national undertaking will be most effective if it is concentrated upon London;

(e) it would be better to have one great National Museum than a multiplicity of lesser ones;

(f) more people would visit such a museum in London than elsewhere (however, this might apply less forcefully if its site should be remote from central London);

(g) if a London museum were developed within existing buildings, these could serve virtually at once as a national collecting-point for important material (however, it seems likely that one or more regional schemes could offer the same facility).

To our minds, the decisive consideration is this: there are thriving and efficient conservation endeavours afoot in various regions of Britain, in the very places where the materials or monuments to be conserved exist; let something at least be done to assist what is already going forward, and after that the wisdom of a totally new venture may be examined.

Great Britain is endeavouring to develop her technology and industry as rapidly as possible. Plans were announced in April for sweeping changes in the North of England and Scotland as a result of the Hunt Committee's study of the so-called "grey areas". This adds yet more weight to the often expressed view that preservation of technical history must be pursued vigorously and quickly if what has been achieved so far is to reach the logical and highly desirable conclusion which the country that gave birth to the technological age so obviously deserves. Vast amounts of money will be spent on Britain's technological future; surely a fraction of this amount could be spent on her past?

Dr R. A. Buchanan (Bath University of Technology)

Sir Arthur Elton, Bt (Chairman of the Council of the Centre for the Study of Industrial Archaeology at Bath University)

Mrs Jane Fawcett (Victorian Society)

Sir David Follett (Science Museum)

Professor A. Rupert Hall (Imperial College)

Dr M. B. Hall (Imperial College)

Mr J. Pope-Hennessy, C.B.E. (Victoria and Albert Museum)

Professor Jack Simmons (University of Leicester)

Dr Norman A. F. Smith (Imperial College)

Mr Rex Wailes (Industrial Monuments Survey)

APPENDIX I

Technological Preservation in the Bath–Bristol Region

by
R. A. Buchanan

The term "Bath–Bristol region" is taken here to describe the river basin of the Bristol Avon below and including the Limpley Stoke valley, stretching northwards into Gloucestershire as far as Little Avon River and southwards into Somersetshire to the southern edge of the Mendip plateau and, in some cases, a little beyond. It is the region which has been dominated for many centuries by the commerce and industry of the twin cities of Bristol and Bath, and particularly by the former which out-stripped Bath in size and importance early in the Middle Ages, largely because of its advantages as a port. The region is, indeed, identical with that which has been described elsewhere as the "Bristol region",* which is a reasonable abbreviation considering the traditional rôle of Bristol as "the metropolis of the West".

The region has fostered many industries in the last millenium, showing a continuity and variety second only to London in the industrial history of the country. As industries have come and gone they have left their marks on the landscape and these have been assimilated or obliterated in successive stages of development. Although Bristol lagged in the rate of industrialization in the nineteenth century, compared with newer and more rapidly growing towns in the Midlands and the North, its growth in absolute terms was high, and the region was strongly influenced by industrial and transport developments in this period. The relics of these nineteenth-century developments are now particularly vulnerable to the processes of industrial modernization and urban renewal, and there has been a remarkably high wastage rate amongst them in recent years. 1968 alone saw the destruction of two outstanding industrial monuments in the inner Bristol area—the *Great Western Cotton Factory* and the *Redcliff Shot Tower*. Two other significant struc-

---

* See R. A. Buchanan and Neil Cossons: *Industrial Archaeology of the Bristol Region* (1969), for a detailed account and for grid references to the location of sites.

tures on the periphery of the region disappeared—the *Sharpness Railway Bridge* and the *Sudbrook pumping engines*. Apart from the battery of six Cornish beam engines at Sudbrook, the loss of which was unnecessary, no convincing case for preserving these structures could be made in the face of the need for new roads, houses, and so on, but it is to be hoped that they have been adequately recorded for posterity. In addition to these major industrial monuments, a host of minor features have vanished in the recent past: toll houses, coal mine buildings, metal working sites, warehouses and railways have all sustained heavy casualties. The need to devise a realistic preservation policy has become most urgent if even a small representative selection of nineteenth-century artefacts is to be retained intact.

The Inner Bristol Area

It will be convenient to consider the industrial remains of the region under three geographical headings: the Inner Bristol area, South Gloucestershire, and North Somerset. Beginning with Bristol, which as the industrial "core" of the region has most to offer, there are currently two critical preservation issues: *Old Temple Meads* and the *Floating Harbour*. Old Temple Meads is the oldest mainline terminus in the world to survive relatively intact. It is intimately associated with the work of its designer, I. K. Brunel, and with local and national history, and its preservation should be above debate. Unfortunately, the future of the station is by no means certain, as the timber-roofed train shed impedes redevelopment of the site by British Rail and the office block fronting on Temple Gate stands in the course of a new road scheme devised by the City Planning Committee. The Floating Harbour is an entirely different sort of industrial monument. This enclosed stretch of high-level water was created at the beginning of the nineteenth century around the tidal wharves of the traditional port of Bristol in the centre of the city. The Port of Bristol Authority (PBA) has now announced that it plans to run down the City Docks of the Floating Harbour over the next ten years, after which it will become redundant and the city will have either to cover it or find an alternative use for it. Powerful amenity arguments may be advanced for preserving the Floating Harbour, but the major difficulty, as so often in such cases, is likely to be the high cost of maintenance. The sympathetic treatment of the Floating Harbour involves many significant features associated with it: *Bristol Bridge*; the wharves of *Welsh Back, The Grove*, and the *River Frome*; *Bathurst Basin*; the *Great Western Dock* (where the *Great Britain* was built by Brunel, and to which the hulk of the ship could conveniently return if enough people can find the imagination and the funds to bring it back); the *Albion Shipyard*; the *Underfall* and *Underfall Yard*; and the *Cumberland Basin* (including *Brunel's Lock, Brunel's Bridges, Old Junction Lock, New Entrance Lock*, and *New Junction Lock* with the original *Hydraulic Power Station* beside it). Outside the Floating Harbour, but still associated with it, are: the *New Cut* (especially the bridges—*Ashton Swing Bridge, Vauxhall Footbridge, Wapping Suspension Footbridge*); the *engineering workshops* at the Underfall Yard (including a range of Whitworth machines dating from the 1880s and a Tangye twin-cylinder horizontal engine of the same period, and also the present *Hydraulic Engine House*); and, downriver from the Floating Harbour itself, *Sea Mills Dock* and the *Powder House*. With the increasing concentration of the activity of the port of Bristol at the mouth of the Avon, the time has come for a complete reassessment of the rôle of the Floating Harbour in the future landscape of the city. It would be a great pity if Bristol lost the stretches of water and maritime activity at its heart which have traditionally been amongst the most distinctive features of the city.

Old Temple Meads and the Floating Harbour are the two most critical preservation issues in Bristol at present. But there are many other nineteenth-century monuments which might "go critical" at any time, and which therefore need to be considered for some form of protection as soon as possible. They include *Clifton Suspension Bridge*; *Clifton Observatory* (the only surviving windmill relic in the city); the remaining Victorian commercial buildings in the exotic "Bristol Byzantine" style, of which *Pearce's Granary* on Welsh Back is the finest example, but *Wills' Old Tobacco Factory*, now derelict on Redcliff Street, should also be considered; the *Tobacco Bond Warehouses* at Cumberland Basin; *Christopher Thomas's Soap Factory* in Broad Plain; the *Coach Factory* at 104 Stokes Croft; *Fullers' Carriage Works* on St George's Road, behind the Council House; *Bush's Warehouse* on Prince Street, in the earlier and more austere style than "Bristol Byzantine" but still characteristically Bristolian; *Canon's Marsh Gas Works*, now largely derelict; *Stapleton Road Gas Works*, if only for its range of steam engines; the *Original Municipal Electricity Generating Station* on Temple Back; the *Tramways Generating Station* on the Counterslip, now incorporated into Courages' Brewery; the stump of a *glass cone* on Redcliff Hill, the only remaining fragment of this once important industry; the two remaining *beehive pottery kilns* at the Bristol Pottery on Lodge Causeway, although the Pottery itself is about to close down; *Trooper's Hill chimney* and the adjacent open ground overlooking the chemical works and other industries of the Crew's Hole valley; the *snuff mill* at Stapleton Glen, the only substantial fragment of a once numerous series of water-mills on the Bristol Frome; *Arnos Castle*, a bizarre building constructed largely from copper slag blocks which were a by-product of the local brass industry; various *turnpike road* relics, such as the *finger-post* at Totterdown (at the forking of the Bath and Wells roads) and the *toll house* at Ashton Gate; railway monuments, such as the *Bristol and Exeter Railway offices* at Temple Meads, and even *New Temple Meads*, which deserves more than a passing glance; *Clifton Rocks Railway*; *Canon's Marsh railway terminal*, an early specimen of reinforced concrete construction; *Brunel House* behind College Green, built to accommodate passengers between train and ship *en route* for New York; and the *tram depot* at Brislington, the largest remnant of the Bristol Tram network which was abandoned in 1941.

The South Gloucestershire Area

Industrial monuments are not so thick on the ground here as they are in Bristol, but there are still a considerable number, particularly connected with the now obsolete Bristol Coalfield and the various transport systems. The relics of the *Avon & Gloucestershire Railway* are specially worthy of attention, including large cuttings, embankments, and a tunnel, built as a coal tramway in 1832. Many tramway and railway alignments survive: for example, the approaches to the pier at *New Passage*, where railway passengers could embark for Wales before the opening of the *Severn Tunnel*, itself a feature of no small interest. Also associated with the tramway system is the curious survival of a rare "*haystack boiler*" in a wood near Westerleigh. The hinterland of Bristol merges gradually into the Gloucestershire woollen industrial region, with important textile mill sites at *Lower Charfield, Upper Charfield*, and *Kingswood*, on the Little Avon River. On the same river at *Huntingford Mill* an overshot water-wheel was at work until recently grinding animal food. There are windmill sites at *Falfield* and *Frampton Cotterell*, and the latter village also has the remains of important *iron mines*, now Water Works property, and a *hat factory* built by Christy & Co. of London in 1818. *Warmley Brass Works* was one of the largest industrial enterprises in the country when it was established in the eighteenth century, although little remains on the site now except an administrative block and the house built by the proprietor, William Champion, now occupied by Warmley RDC. The factory was taken over by *Warmley Pottery* for the manufacture of industrial earthenware, but this has now also closed although the firm still operates in another factory on the north side of Warmley. The village of Warmley is in the middle of the ancient Kingswood Coalfield, which was worked intensively for many centuries until the first half of the present century, but this long tradition of coal working has left surprisingly few industrial monuments. Another local industry has been the manufacture of brick and tile: there is a derelict *brickworks* at Shortwood, but the large firm at *Cattybrook* is still in production. Limestone quarrying is still a big industry around Yate, where celestine is also worked. Again, however, there are no distinctive industrial monuments. The *turnpike roads* have left a good scattering of relics across the area in the shape of milestones and toll houses, although one of the nicest of the local toll houses was recently demolished at *Rangeworthy*.

The North Somersetshire Area

Like the Bristol Coalfield north of the Avon, the Somerset coal-producing districts are rapidly becoming obsolete, leaving only two active mines (*Kilmersdon* and *Writhlingdon*) at Radstock. The North Somerset Coalfield, indeed, has reverted with remarkable rapidity to a rural landscape, spoil heaps being removed for road-making or becoming covered with vegetation, and the old mining villages being adapted as commuters' dormitory settlements. In their hey-day, however, the coal mines encouraged the construction of important canals of which there are some significant remains: the *Kennet & Avon Canal*, with notable features at *Widcombe Locks*, the *iron bridges* at Widcombe and Sydney Gardens, *Claverton pumping engine*, and *Dundas* and *Avoncliffe aqueducts*; the *Somersetshire Coal Canal*, starting at *Dundas Basin* and going up the Midford valley via the *Combe Hay Locks* to the *Summit Basin* at Goosard Bridge; and the *Dorset & Somerset Canal*, which was never completed, although sections of the Nettle-bridge Branch were constructed and survive at *Coleford Aqueduct*, *Mells Lock Pits*, and *Murtry Aqueduct*. Metal working in North Somerset is well represented by industrial monuments: the lead smelting plant which survives in ruins on the Mendip plateau at *Charterhouse, Priddy* and *Smitham Hill*; the derelict edge-tool factory of Fussells in a wooded valley near *Mells*; the copper mill now converted to other uses at *Swineford*; and the ruinous brass works on the Avon at *Keynsham, Saltford* and *Kelston*. An important extractive industry in the area, in addition to coal, was stone—particularly the freestone mined and quarried on the hills around Bath—and remnants of the tramways which connected these workings with the roads and canals in the valleys may be found at *Bathampton, Conkwell* and *Winsley*. Paper is still manu-factured in the area at *Bathford* and at *Wookey Hole*, and the derelict *De Montalt Mill* still stands at Combe Down, Bath (this once boasted the largest water-wheel in England, but it does not survive). Other important water-mills still exist at *Albert Mill*, Keynsham, until recently grinding logwood for dyes; *Dunkirk Mill, Freshford*, one of several woollen mill sites on or near the Somerset Frome; *Priston Mill*, used on a farm for agricultural purposes, with a large overshot wheel still in working order; and *Chew Magna*, where a water-mill grinds animal feed. There is also a handful of windmill sites, including *Brockley Combe, Uphill*, *Worlebury* and *Felton*, but the prize specimen is the handsomely restored mill at *Chapel Allerton*. Beyond the limits of the Bath–Bristol region, there are important groups of mills in Bradford-on-Avon, Trowbridge and Frome, representing the most important surviving features of the West of England woollen cloth industry: many of these have been converted to other uses, notably the premises in Bradford occupied since the middle of the nineteenth century by a rubber-manufacturing firm which still possesses some of its original machinery such as the "Iron Duke", a calendering machine. *Turnpike* relics are scattered over the area, with a con-centration around Bath associated with the *Bath Turnpike Trust* (note especially the good sets of milestones and the distinctive *terminus stones*). *Railway* remains include the alignment and attendant debris of the *Somerset & Dorset Railway*, with *Bath*

Green Park Station still intact as a car park. The main Paddington–Bristol line sweeps through the area, with important Brunel remains at the *Box Tunnel, Bath Spa Station*, and the *viaduct* out of Bath through Twerton. The City of Bath has two important footbridges: *Victoria Bridge*, designed by Dredge on an unusual suspension pattern, and *Widcombe Bridge*, a girder bridge which replaced a previous wooden structure after its tragic collapse in 1877. Another iron structure in the area which celebrated its centenary in 1969 is the *pier* at Clevedon. North Somerset contains the major reservoirs of Bristol Water Works at Blagdon and Chew Lake, with storage and treatment plant at Barrow Gurney: important associated industrial monuments survive in the shape of steam engines preserved at *Blagdon* and *Chelvey* (there is another BWW steam engine at *Victoria Pumping Station* in Clifton). *Bath Gas Works* has an impressive battery of steam engines still at work in its North Engine House. Glass was produced in Nailsea on a large scale early in the nineteenth century but little remains of *Nailsea Glass Works* although a few surface features survive of the local coalfield amongst the desirable residences of the dormitory village, especially the *Cornish Engine House* at Backwell Colliery.

Conclusion: The Problems of Preservation

A survey such as this is bound to be selective if it is not to become too long and tedious. It is to be hoped that this list of industrial monuments requiring sympathetic treatment has not transgressed too far over the acceptable tolerance of tedium, but it is necessary to indicate the main features of the scene in order to make realistic suggestions regarding preservation.

(1) An *ad hoc* preservation policy has been in operation for the region during the past five years because of the initiative of Bristol City Museum (BCM) under its Director, Mr Alan Warhurst, and the Curator in Technology, Mr Neil Cossons. This policy has consisted of looking at everything movable which has become available for preservation, and taking as much as possible for the Museum. It has extended to large pieces of machinery such as the *Old Mills winding engine* but it has not applied to immovable structures such as the ill-fated *Redcliff Shot Tower*, with the significant exception of the buildings, including *Stratford Water-mill*, re-erected in the grounds of Blaise Castle Park, and the elegant windmill at *Chapel Allerton* donated to BCM by Mr C. C. Clarke in

1966. The Museum policy has been supported by Bristol Industrial Archaeological Society (BIAS) and by the Centre for the Study of the History of Technology (CSHT) at Bath University of Technology, which have helped to keep open lines of communication and to enable action to be taken quickly when the need has arisen.

(2) The CSHT has also co-operated with the Bristol City Museum in the preservation of Western Region British Railway documents—mainly engine and rolling stock part drawings—which had been declared redundant by BR. The offer of these documents came as a result of an initiative by Sir Arthur Elton. They were removed from the offices at Swindon and are now stored in the Bristol City Museum where they await sorting and classification. On the sample taken so far it does not appear that anything of value has been allowed to leave BR. But at least a precedent has been set and a procedure devised for dealing with redundant industrial documents in the region, even if the facilities for this sort of storage which can be offered by the Bristol City Museum are limited.

(3) The movable material and documents collected by BCM are at present in a store awaiting the long-delayed construction of a new museum in Bristol. The store is already overcrowded, and it will soon become necessary to consider the acquisition of further store space, which may prove to be administratively difficult. The Council of the CSHT did consider some time ago the possibility of establishing a regional "dump" for technological material, but the idea was dropped largely because it was felt that a region with an alert museum did not require such a service, while a region without such a museum was unlikely to support one: in either case the initiative (or lack of it) of the regional museum seemed to be the crucial factor.

(4) The points made so far relate to movable material and documents, in which museums have a dominant rôle to play. Immovable monuments present a different set of problems, in response to which experience in the Bath–Bristol region has emphasized certain points:

(a) It is hopeless trying to preserve large structures unless some use can be found for them. *Pearce's Granary* and *Bush's Warehouse*, for example, cannot be kept empty without maintenance indefinitely, and it was a stroke of good fortune for the preservationists when Acker Bilk took a lease on the Granary for his Jazz

Club. Bush's has not yet been so fortunate, and as an empty and perforce decaying shell it becomes increasingly vulnerable to those, such as the City Planning Committee, who want to put a new road through it. The same functional problem destroyed the case for preserving the *Great Western Cotton Factory* and weakens alarmingly the case for *Old Temple Meads*. The ideal solution for the latter would have been to convert it *in toto* into a museum, but this cut across accepted BCM policy and structural alterations at the main-line end of the station have now made this less attractive: meanwhile, the train shed remains as a car park and the superstructure gets increasingly dilapidated.

(b) A related problem to that of utility is the financial problem. We have not been very fortunate so far in raising money for industrial monuments in the region, although we have not yet put the public response to the test of an appeal, partly because of the great number and variety of monuments requiring attention. We are concerned at the erosion of objects such as the Avon valley brass works, the Mendip lead smelting sites, and the Combe Hay locks on the Somersetshire Coal Canal: erosion caused by weather (including the dramatic floods of last July), vegetation, and vandalism. But we have not yet managed to prevent this. Useful clues as to what might be done are provided by the Kennet & Avon Canal Trust and the Somerset County Council School Field Centre at Charterhouse on Mendip, both of which use voluntary labour on valuable restoration and excavation work. It would be possible to think in terms of Amenity Centres manned initially by voluntary labour at places such as Priddy lead works, Kelston brass works, and even a derelict colliery like that at New Rock. But these schemes would require a lot of money at a fairly early stage, and as yet this is not forthcoming.

(c) An even more delicate problem is that of ownership, because an unsympathetic owner can make preservation virtually impossible. Few of the owners of important industrial monuments in the Bath–Bristol region are blessed with this vital imaginative quality: the general view seems to be that such-and-such a monument can be left until the land is wanted and then it will have to go. The two most important owners in the region come into this category—British Rail and the City Planning Committee. BR ambivalence and unimaginativeness was responsible for the quite unnecessary destruction of the Sudbrook engines, and the desire of

BR to redevelop the Old Temple Meads site ensures that, if the fate of the structure is left to that organization, it will be left to fall down—to the general satisfaction of the owners. The City Fathers are equally failing in imaginative sympathy regarding the Temple Gate frontage of Old Temple Meads and, one fears, for the future of the Floating Harbour. On the credit side in this respect, some enterprises have responded in an encouraging manner to the discovery that they are responsible for important industrial monuments: Bristol Water Works, for example, has preserved several steam engines, and the PBA is proud of its extraordinary collection of machines in its Underfall Yard Workshops. Even here, however, changes in management or ownership (e.g. the possible nationalization of the docks) may lead to sudden changes of policy and the loss of irreplaceable monuments, so that even the best-intentioned enterprises require supervision by an independent body.

(5) The bodies concerned with the preservation of industrial monuments in the Bath–Bristol region are moving slowly towards a coherent policy for preserving a representative selection of industrial monuments. While the BCM continues its policy of emergency rescues (it is to be hoped that the "Iron Duke" from Bradford-on-Avon will be one of its acquisitions in the immediate future), a list of sites along the lines of the survey in the first part of this paper is being prepared for adequate scheduling by the Ministry of Public Buildings and Works and whatever other forms of protection may seem appropriate. In the last resort, however, the success of any such policy will rely upon the support of public opinion, which must be aroused to an awareness of the importance of industrial monuments as part of the cultural heritage and amenity-value of the region. By a sustained pressure of such an enlightened public opinion it would be possible to persuade owners to look after industrial monuments in their care, to raise money for Trusts and amenity-schemes in order to restore and preserve industrial monuments, and, perhaps, to find suitable uses for those large monuments which become an embarrassment when they are left empty. Widespread public support for the objectives of technological preservation is thus the most pressing end towards which we must work.

APPENDIX II

Technological collections in Great Britain

This list includes museums and collections having technological material, even if only a single item. It is not claimed that the list is complete. Technological material may be found in many county and city museums not listed here.

Museum or collection	Topics covered
Aberdeen	
Alexander Price & Sons	Paper
Alton	
Curtis Museum	Agriculture plus a Columbian printing press
Ashford	
Wye College of Agriculture Museum	Agriculture
Bangor	
Penrhyn Castle	Transport, industry and agriculture
Barnard Castle	
Bowes Museum	Industry of the North-East (in store)
Basingstoke	
Willis Museum	Horology plus Basingstoke Canal navigation
Batley	
Bagshaw Museum	Textile industry
Battle	
Battle Museum	Sussex iron industry
Beaulieu	
Maritime Museum	Ship exhibits
Montagu Motor Museum	Road transport
Bedford	
Bedford Museum	Bicycles, typewriters, sewing machines, communications

Museum or collection	*Topics covered*
Belfast	
Transport Museum	All aspects
Ulster Folk Museum	Farms, mills, small industries
Ulster Museum	Textiles, flax and linen, cycles, horology
Bideford	
Bideford Museum	Shipwright's tools
Biggleswade	
Shuttleworth Collection	Aviation and road transport
Bilston	
Branch Library, Museum, Art Gallery	Local industry, iron and steel
Birmingham	
Assay Office	Library, silverware, Boulton & Watt material
Avery Historical Museum	Weighing
Museum of Science and Industry	General
Blackburn	
Blackburn Museum	Horology
Lewis Museum	Textiles
Blandford	
Royal Signals Museum	Army communications
Bolton	
Tonge Moor Museum	Textiles
Bournemouth	
Rothesay Museum	Maritime, armour
Russell-Cotes Art Gallery and Museum	Reference collection of trams, trolley buses and railways
Bradford	
Bolling Hall	Textiles
Cartwright Hall	Transport, textiles, photography, radio, typewriters
Brentford	
British Piano Museum	Musical instruments
Brighton	
Creed & Co. Ltd	Telecommunications and transport

Museum or collection	*Topics covered*
Bristol	
City Museum	Local industry and transport
Britton & Sons	Shoe making
Harvey's Ltd	Wine making
Bristol Waterworks Co.	Waterworks equipment
Blaise Castle	Water-mill
Brixham	
Brixham Museum	Maritime navigation, fishing
Broadway	
Snowshill Manor	Horology, ship models, instruments
Buckland Abbey	
Buckland Abbey	Maritime, agriculture, building
Budleigh Salterton	
Bicton Countryside Museum	Agriculture, cider making, traction engines
Bury St Edmunds	
Gershom-Parkington Memorial Collection	Horology
Camberley	
National Army Museum	Militaria
Camborne	
Holman Museum	Mining
Cardiff	
National Museum of Wales	Welsh industry, coal mining
South Wales Electricity Board	Electrical
Carlisle	
Carr's Biscuit Works	Food technology
Cowans Sheldon Ltd	Cranes
Cummersdale Print Works	Printing
Castletown	
Nautical Museum	Maritime
Cheddar	
Motor Museum	Transport
Chelmsford	
Chelmsford and Essex Museum	Local industry
Crompton Parkinson	Electrical

Museum or collection	*Topics covered*
Cheltenham	
Skyframe Aircraft Museum	Aviation
Clayton-Le-Moors	
Mercer Museum	Coal
Coalbrookdale (see *Ketley*)	
Colchester	
Colchester and Essex Museum	Photography and instruments
Davey Paxman & Co.	Pumping engine
Coventry	
Herbert Art Gallery and Museum	Various
Cranfield	
College of Aeronautics	Aviation
Cregneash	
Manx Folk Museum	Rural techniques
Crich	
Tramway Museum	Transport
Darlington	
Darlington Museum	Transport and local industry
Derby	
Derby Museum	Transport, local industry
Dudley	
Samuel Lewis & Co.	Nails
Dundee	
City Museum	Whaling
Barrack Street Museum	Shipping and local industry
Eastbourne	
Royal National Lifeboat Institution Museum	Lifeboats and equipment
Eccles	
Monks Hall Museum	Nasmyth machine tools
Edinburgh	
National Museum	Agriculture and early technology
Royal Scottish Museum	General
The *Scotsman* office	Picture telegraph receiver
Transport Museum	Public road transport
Gainsborough	
Rose Bros Albion Works	Wrapping machines

Museum or collection	*Topics covered*
Glamis	
Angus Folk Museum	Local industry, agriculture, textiles
Glasgow	
Art Gallery and Museum	Maritime
Museum of Transport	Transport
Gloucester	
Folk Life and Regimental Museum	Agriculture, local industry, Severn fishing and transport
Great Yarmouth	
Maritime Museum for East Anglia	Maritime
Greenock	
McLean Museum	Maritime, Watt engine
Halifax	
Bankfield Museum	Textiles
Shibden Hall Folk Museum	Agriculture, transport
Harrow	
Kodak Museum	Photography
Hartlebury	
Worcestershire County Museum	Local industry, transport, textiles
Hartlepool	
Gray Art Gallery and Museum	Maritime, timber, salt
Hastings	
Public Museum	Sussex ironwork
Museum of Local History	Ship models
Hawick	
Wilton Lodge Museum	Textiles, knitting machinery
Hayes	
E.M.I. Museum	Audio techniques
Helmshore	
Museum of Early Textile Machines	Textiles
Helston	
Helston Borough Museum	Agriculture and fire appliances
Henlow	
Royal Air Force Museum	Aviation (not yet open)

Museum or collection	*Topics covered*
Hertford	
Hertford Museum	Local industry
High Wycombe	
Museum and Exhibition Room	Chairs
Parker-Knoll Ltd	Chairs
Huddersfield	
Tolson Memorial Museum	Local industry, textiles
Hull	
Maritime Museum	Maritime
Transport Museum	Road vehicles
Hull Corporation Water Department	Cornish engine plus other equipment
Keighley	
Cliffe Castle Museum	Hand crafts, weights and measures, radio and telegraphy, "Wankel" engine of 1909
Ketley	
Coalbrookdale Works Museum	Iron and steel
Kidderminster	
West Midlands Gas Board	Gas equipment
Kingston-upon-Thames	
Kingston-upon-Thames Museum	Photography
Kingussie	
Highland Folk Museum	Agriculture
Lackham	
Lackham School of Agriculture	Agriculture
Lancaster	
Lancaster City Museum	Local industry, maritime, communications
Leamington	
G. R. Southorn	Shoe making
Leeds	
Leeds City Museum	Prime movers, transport
Abbey House Museum	Local industry

Museum or collection	*Topics covered*
Leicester	
Imperial Typewriter Co.	Typewriters
Leicester Museum and Art Gallery	Technology of the East Midlands, transport
Leigh	
Pennington Hall Museum	Textiles
Lincoln	
Ruston & Hornsby Ltd	Transport, stationary engines
Usher Gallery	Watches
Museum of Lincolnshire Life	Agricultural industry (not yet open)
Little Rissington	
Central Flying School Museum	Aviation
Liverpool	
Chadberns Ltd	Instruments
Clay & Abraham Ltd	Chemist's equipment
Morath Bros	Clocks
Tate & Lyle Ltd	Sugar refining
Rushworth & Dreaper	Musical instruments
City of Liverpool Museum	Transport, shipping, especially models
Llanelli	
Steel Company of Wales	Tin-plate
London	
Clockmakers' Company	Horology
Dollond & Aitchison Ltd	Optics and instruments
Danor Engineering Ltd	Clothes irons
Meltonian Wren Ltd	Footwear
Museum of British Transport	Rail and road vehicles
National Maritime Museum	Maritime; *Cutty Sark*
Post Office Permanent Telecommunications Exhibition	Telecommunications
The Rotunda	Artillery and small arms
Imperial War Museum	Military technology
Science Museum	Everything
Television Gallery	T.V. history
R. White & Sons	Mineral water bottles
Greenwich Borough Museum	Local commerce and industry

Museum or collection	*Topics covered*
London (Colney)	
DH Mosquito Museum	Aviation
Looe	
The Cornish Museum	Mining and fishing
Luton	
Vauxhall Motors Ltd	Motor cars
Maidstone	
Tyrwhitt Drake Museum of Carriages	Road transport
Manchester	
Ferranti Ltd	Electrical
Museum of Science and Technology	General (newly opened)
Newcastle-upon Tyne	
Museum of Science and Engineering	General
Museum of Department of Mining Engineering at University of Newcastle	Mining
Newport	
Carisbrooke Castle Museum	Donkey wheel, Marconi records
Northampton	
Central Museum	Shoe-making machinery
Norwich	
Bridewell Museum	Many local industries
Laurence, Scott & Electromotors	Electric motors
Nottingham	
Nottingham Industrial Museum	Local technologies including lace making and knitting machines (to be opened)
Ericsson Telephones	Telephony (not open to the public)
Raleigh Industries Ltd	Bicycles (not open to the public)
Oxford	
Morris Motors Ltd	Early motor cars
University Press	Printing

Museum or collection	*Topics covered*
Pickering	
Beck Isle Museum	Wheelwrighting, fairground machines
Plymouth	
City Museum	Industrial arts
Polegate	
Wilmington Priory Museum	Agriculture
Poole	
Poole Museum	Maritime, industrial archaeology
Portmadoc	
Festiniog Railway	Rail transport
Portsmouth	
Eastney Pump House	Steam pumps
Victory Museum	H.M.S. *Victory*
Reading	
Museum of English Rural Life	Agriculture and farm technology
Rochdale	
John Holroyd & Co.	Beam engine, 1841
Rochester	
Public Museum	Ship and sea-plane models
Rotherham	
Rotherham Corporation	Weighing and measuring
Guest & Crimes Ltd	Old water meters
St Albans	
City Museum	Craft tools
St Helens	
Pilkington Glass Museum	Glass making
St Ives	
Barnes Museum	Cinematography
St Mary Cray	
National Paper Museum	Paper making (in store)
Salford	
Science Museum	Coal mining, local industry
Saltcoats	
North Ayrshire Museum	Local industry
Sheffield	
Abbeydale Industrial Hamlet	Steel working
Shepherd Wheel	Water-powered grinding shop

Museum or collection	*Topics covered*
Shoreham-on-Sea	
Marlipins Museum	Maritime
Shugborough	
Staffs. County Museum	Mining, iron, glass making, chemical engineering, transport (site under development)
Southend on-Sea	
Historic Aircraft Museum	Aviation (not yet open)
South Shields	
South Shields Museum	Local glass, maritime
Stoke Bruerne	
Waterways Museum	Canal transport
Stoke Prior	
Avoncroft Museum	Building technology
Street	
C. & J. Clark Ltd	Shoe making
Stroud	
Stroud Museum	Local industry
Sunderland	
Sunderland Museum	Maritime, stationary and railway engines, illumination, various others
Swansea	
Industrial Museum of South Wales	Local industry, nickel, tin, oil refining
Swindon	
G.W.R. Museum	Railway locomotives
Garrard Engineering Co., Ltd	Early gramophone equipment
Taunton	
Somerset County Museum	Stationary engines, electrical equipment
Post Office Collection	Early telephone equipment
Totnes	
Elizabethan House	Local crafts, Babbage material, transport
Towyn	
Narrow Gauge Railway Museum	Transport

Museum or collection	*Topics covered*
Truro	
County Museum (Royal Institution of Cornwall)	Mining and mineralogy
Wareham	
Royal Armoured Corps Tank Museum	Armoured fighting vehicles
Weston-Super-Mare	
Yieldingtree Railway Museum	Transport
Whitby	
Whitby Museum	Shipbuilding, whaling and mining
Willenhall	
J. Parkes & Sons Ltd	Locks
Wilmington	
Wilmington Museum	Agriculture
Winchester	
Westgate Museum	Weights and measures, local pieces
Wolverhampton	
Chubb & Sons	Locks and safes (not open to the public)
Yeovilton	
Fleet Air Arm Museum	Naval aviation
York	
Castle Museum	Hand crafts, domestic appliances, transport, water-driven corn-mill
Railway Museum	Transport
Zennor	
Wayside Museum	Mining, quarrying, agriculture

APPENDIX III

Two examples of preservation by means of Private Trusts

I. The Finch Foundry Trust

The Finch Foundry is at Sticklepath near Okehampton. From 1814 until 1960 members of the Finch family ran the Foundry and produced high quality agricultural tools such as scythes, shovels and billhooks. Mass production and increasing farm mechanization forced the firm out of business after 1960.

The Foundry was water-powered by means of three wheels, one to drive a pair of "trip" hammers, another to act as a "blowing" engine for the forges and the third to power grindstones and finishing tools. The three wheels were fed from the River Taw.

After its abandonment as a commercial proposition the Finch Foundry became derelict, but because most of the machinery survived and because it is so well known in the South-West, a charitable trust was set up to raise money and to arrange the restoration and protection of the buildings and equipment.

The Trust publicized its intentions locally through newspapers and nationally by means of a two-page illustrated leaflet which was circulated through individuals and societies and also via such publications as *Industrial Archaeology* and the *Newcomen Bulletin*. People were invited to help in five ways:

1. By making a donation either in money or in building materials such as timber or concrete.
2. By forming or joining a team of voluntary workers to work on the project.
3. By helping the Trustees to organize the available funds, men and materials.
4. By collecting examples of Finch tools to display in a museum.
5. By making the project known to other people.

A great deal of help was forthcoming from influential individuals such as Mr Rex Wailes, Mr Kenneth Hudson and Mr J. L. E. Smith, M.P. and also from such organizations as The Newcomen Society, The Society for the Protection of Ancient Buildings, The Pilgrim Trust, St Luke's College in Exeter, Messrs Lavering, Pochin & Co. Ltd, and English Clays.

The appeal was successful and the Finch Foundry is now operational and open to the public.

II. *The Cheddleton Flint Mill Preservation Trust*

The Cheddleton Flint Mill is on the River Churnet in North Staffordshire. In the eighteenth century the pottery industry began to use flint in their earthenware in order to improve its whiteness. The very hard flint was first burnt in kilns, then crushed and then ground between four heavy stone blocks pushed round in a circle by rotating arms and a fixed stone pavement. This type of flint mill was usually driven by a water-wheel and the one at Cheddleton is the only surviving example.

In order to preserve the Cheddleton Flint Mill a Preservation Trust was set up in May 1967 by the following people:

Professor S. H. Beaver (Professor of Geography at the University of Keele)
Mr Robert Copeland (China manufacturer)
Mr Charles Hawell (Member of the Newcomen Society)
Mr Arnold Mountford (Director of Stoke-on-Trent City Museum)
Mr Derek Prall (Local businessman)
Mr Rex Wailes (Consultant to the Industrial Monuments Survey)

In October 1967 the Trust was registered as a charity, a non-profit making concern. It is of interest to set out the details of the cost of preserving the mill in working order, opening it to the public and setting up a museum of the ceramic milling industry.

	£
Purchase of mill	1,400
Building repairs	670
Materials for repairs to wheels and equipment	550
Fencing for public's safety	180
Lighting and power installations	260
Extra items	200
Display cases, etc.	170
Cost of paint, trees, shrubs, seats, tools and equipment to maintain appearance, Bank interest, curator's honorarium, legal charges, rates, etc.	831
	£4,261

The Cheddleton Mill Trust publicized its plans by means of a small illustrated folder which was circulated through individuals and the *Newcomen Bulletin*. The Trust appealed for financial contributions and on request made available a Deed of Covenant form, a device which is frequently used by preservation trusts in order to encourage the maximum amount of financial help.

The restoration work is not yet complete but already one of the wheels is operational and on 19 April 1969 the Cheddleton Flint Mill was opened to the public.

APPENDIX IV

The major Technological Museums
under development

The Black Country

The proposal is for a Museum of Black Country Folk Life and Industrial History.

> Mr R. S. G. Traves
> Libraries, Museums and Arts Department
> Central Library
> St James's Road
> Dudley
> Worcestershire

Bristol

The City Museum plans a Department of Technology for which many exhibits are now in store.

> The Curator of Technology
> Bristol City Museum
> Queen's Road
> Bristol, 8

East Midlands

A Museum of Technology for the East Midlands is planned for a site in the City of Leicester. Some items are on temporary exhibition; the rest are in store. The Secretary of the Steering Committee is:

> Mr T. A. Walden
> Director
> City Museums and Art Gallery
> New Walk
> Leicester

Lea Valley

As part of the Lea Valley Regional Park in east London, there are proposals for a technological museum based on the Abbey Mills Pumping Station.

> Mr D. P. Smith
> 22 Horn Lane
> Woodford Green
> Essex

Manchester

A Museum of Science and Technology is planned for the City of Manchester and a portion of the exhibits are now on temporary display.

> Dr R. L. Hills
> Institute of Science and Technology
> University of Manchester
> P.O. Box No. 88
> Sackville Street
> Manchester, 1

North-East

The Northern Region Open Air Museum will be built at Beamish Hall in County Durham. Very many items have already been stored.

> Mr Frank Atkinson
> The Bowes Museum
> Barnard Castle
> Co. Durham

Telford

Telford New Town will embrace the Ironbridge Gorge Museum which is designed to preserve the industrial and technological history of Coalbrookdale and its environs.

> Mr G. R. Morton
> Department of Applied Science
> Wolverhampton College of Technology
> Wolverhampton